BOB HOPE

First published in Great Britain in 1998 by Chameleon Books
an imprint of André Deutsch Ltd
76 Dean Street
London W1V 5HA

André Deutsch Ltd is a VCI plc company

www.vci.co.uk

Design: Neal Townsend for JMP Ltd
Picture research: Karen Tucker for JMP Ltd

Printed in the UK by Jarrold Book Printing

A catalogue record for this book is available from the British Library

ISBN 0 233 99269 3

BOB HOPE

An Illustrated Biography
Michael Freedland

For Ben and Jamie

Welcome to the world

ACKNOWLEDGMENTS

Writing about Bob Hope was made immeasurably easier by the help of people who knew him so well. So, for talking to me, I must thank with gratitude:

Steve Allen, Carol Baker, the late George Burns, Les Brown, Jeanne Carmen, Phyllis Diller, the late Mel Frank, Lord Grade of Elstree, Hal Kanter, Jan King, Elliot Kozak, Frances Langford, the late Dean Martin, Arthur Marx, Virginia Mayo, Barney McNulty, Janis Paige, the late Norman Panama, Anthony Quinn, Melville Shavelson, Bob Slatzer and Bob Thomas.

Much of the research for this book was conducted at the same time as the preparation of a television programme for the BBC and the American Movie Classics channel. My thanks and admiration are acknowledged to the producer/director Chris Hunt.

Finally, very sincere thanks to my editor, Hannah MacDonald.

Michael Freeland
London, 1998

CONTENTS

Chapter One – THANKS FOR THE MEMORY

They called him America's best-loved comedian. It must have been love, for why else wheel out Bob Hope, at the age of ninety-four, simply, to say a few words in a TV commercial for a supermarket chain? Only love could make an organization that didn't specialize in zimmer frames or incontinence pads automatically think of a man that old for their screen image. But then, the fellow christened Leslie Townes Hope has never been like other men.

From vaudeville, through high-class Broadway review, to Hollywood and then radio and television, he has been brilliantly successful. He has also been a mass of enormous contradictions.

Hope was born, according to the records, on 29 May 1903 at Eltham in south - east London (officially Kent or 'Kent County', as he was to love calling it in his old age). Yet he has all the special affection for the land he adopted that only adopted children have for their legal parents. He took to America and America took to him. He even took on its state religion – golf – and became its high priest.

And then there is contradiction number two: in a profession where comics once wore red noses and loud check suits, Bob Hope dressed in the best styles and had the looks of a matinée idol.

But strangest of all his contradictions is that the man who was the professional coward on screen could spend a whole day surveying the medals that came to him for entertaining troops in the midst of bombs and shells that fell in four wars. (More than once, he and his fellow entertainers would have to duck from enemy fire – at least, that is what they said they were ducking from, although a comedian could never be sure. As he said, he was frequently given a twenty-one-gun salute, 'and at least three of them were ours'.)

It is true that, where there was army life, there was army Hope – and where there was Hope there was usually also an NBC camera ready to feature him on a major TV special, for which he was paid a fantastic sum of money. Nothing, however, should blunt the fact that this wasn't just bravery: it was also a recognition that there were people out there thirsting for the kind of entertainment he had on offer.

Another contradiction is that this man – whose real fame came from reading the tastes of America as well as any chef could judge the palates of his clients – misjudged them so badly in the midst of the Vietnam conflict. He was a hawk at a time when almost everyone else in showbusiness was burning so many draft cards that they had to print more to keep up with the demand.

Hope on duty - just one of the perks of entertaining the troops.

BOB HOPE

Sometimes it got pretty tiring.

For seventy years, he has been a top-flight entertainer, for most of that time richer than almost anyone else in the United States. Everyone says he achieved success through his sense of timing. If that is so, why were people asking if he got that timing wrong at the end? If he shouldn't have stopped and allowed the memories to speak for themselves.

Perhaps part of the answer lies in the fact that this most loved of entertainers was always in the midst of a love affair with his audience. Once, that audience was a group of Navajo Indians, whom Bob had spotted from a bus trudging across the desert.

He told the driver of his bus to stop. 'What for?' asked the driver. 'I want to try out some of my monologue jokes,' said Bob. He did his whole act – eliciting just bemused looks on the faces of the Indians. They got back on to the bus and Bob's writer, Melville Shavelson, taunted him: 'Bob, you wasted all that time, they didn't understand a word.'

Hope, in old, old age – at 93.

Back to his favourite audience. In the Gulf, 1991.

'Yeh,' he said. 'But we had a rehearsal.'

He also had a captive audience. He needed an audience the way other people needed a friendly smile. Sometimes it was just a single pretty girl on a single pretty couch. And that's yet another contradiction for the guy who preached the value of family life, not least that of his own family.

If he were up to discussing such things these days, he would probably say it was just part of the process of being a human being – or being a louse, depending on your way of looking at it.

But the truth of the matter is, no matter what you think of his morals or his thirst for riches, in his heyday he wasn't just a great stage and screen comedian, he was also a pretty good comedy actor – and went on to become one of the funniest men in the world. As he might have said: 'Good evening ladies and gentlemen – this is Bob They-Love-Me-Everywhere-I-Go-And-This-Isn't-Just-A-Memory Hope.' 🅱

Chapter Two – NOW, I WANT TO TELL YA. . .

The question has to be asked: would Leslie Townes Hope have been just as successful had his family stayed in London and not crossed the Atlantic in the steerage section of some ocean-going liner back in 1907?

The answer is difficult to assess, so let's look at the evidence. It wasn't a rags-to-riches story exactly. The family were never totally broke – although it had been lack of money that drove William Hope to Cleveland, Ohio, in the first place. Back in England, what little cash William had from his dwindling stone-cutting business had tended to improve the income of local publicans more than that of his wife Avis. Avis had been born in Wales as Avis Townes, and it was her maiden name that gave Leslie his second given name. Sometimes she got engagements as a concert singer, but there were never enough of them to bring any kind of prosperity to the family.

The family business had been established by William's father James in Hitchin in Hertfordshire, but what had once been a thriving concern – James had been involved in building the Law Courts in London's Strand and later worked on the Statue of Liberty when it was created in Paris – was being run to the ground by his son. They were constantly on the move, first to Eltham and then to Bristol, although the now retired James continued to live in Hitchin.

Emigrating was a last resort. In 1907, William decided there was no future for his family in Britain. He had heard that the skills of fully trained building craftsmen were much in demand in the United States. Just a few months later – it was Christmas – William sent for Avis and her sons.

In Cleveland, they were contented as they had never been before. Two more sons arrived, but a daughter, Emily, died in childhood. The boys went to the local school. The fact that Leslie got only as far as the eighth grade had nothing to do with the family's financial situation. He just didn't like sitting in a classroom. He was already the comedian of the family – and the school. So another question is worth asking: Had he stayed in England, would he have been just as funny?

Of course, no one knows the answer to this, although one can guess. Laughter is infectious, as everyone knows, but being able to *make* people laugh isn't nearly so much a contagion. Only George, the youngest of Leslie's brothers, was known to have anything approaching a sense of humour and both he and the kid Leslie would probably have laughed no matter where they lived. His older siblings – Fred, Ivor, Jim and Jack and his younger brothers George and Sid – all chose

In vaudeville. He could have been a song and dance man.

different ways of making a living, frequently helped to set up businesses by Leslie. George, for a time, worked with him in vaudeville before moving on to something more respectable.

Would Leslie – later Bob – have had the same sort of success if his family had remained in England? He might have done well in the music hall, just like his fellow South Londoner Charlie Chaplin – but he, too, had to go to America to become rich and famous. In his early years in Cleveland, Hope would sneak into the back of a vaudeville theatre and dream of one day being a success, but it was just a dream.

It certainly didn't feature in the aspirations of William Hope, the stonemason. He didn't promise to stop drinking, but he had gone to America because he thought that there was going to be some kind of security. People always died and when they died they always needed funerals and usually they needed tombstones. Also, there was a good chance that new buildings would be needed. He believed that almost as a matter of religious faith. Indeed, William, a member of the Church of England and later its American offshoot, the Episcopalians, became a Presbyterian and his family changed with him – because he was asked to work on a new church for the denomination.

Leslie was to remain a nominal Presbyterian for the rest of his life, although, once he married, he was alone in that affiliation. As his younger daughter would say, 'We're all Catholics in this house, except Daddy – and he's a comedian.'

Indeed, comedy was in the young Hope's blood. Even if William Hope would never know it. *His* favourite entertainment had to be vaudeville, just as in England it had to be the music hall or variety. It has been said that both vaudeville and variety were products of the industrial revolution – the men who sweated and swore at machines and workbenches needed somewhere to let down their hair, an entertainment where they could laugh while they swilled their beer and ogled the girls.

These were not places for the faint-hearted – and certainly not for children. Young Leslie would not have got far in a British music hall. They employed people to kick out kids like him if they had so much as a whiff of the beer and sawdust, to say nothing of the acrid perfume of the performers. But they would have had a great time, seeing Harry Lauder twirling his shillelagh while Hetty King puffed her cigar and Ella Shields sang about being Burlington Bertie from Bow – and all for twopence in the gallery.

In America, in the old two-a-day (two performances a day, although there were sometimes seven or eight), performers like the Howard Brothers and Smith and Dale, and later on George Burns and Gracie Allen and Jack Benny – to say nothing of Powe's Elephants, Fink's Mules and Swayne's Cats and Rats – did the same act year in, year out, gradually and comfortably going from place to place with a routine that present-day TV would eat alive in one hour.

Leslie loved the idea of entertaining, much more than he loved the idea of school. At the age of 12, he entered a talent contest as Charlie Chaplin. He would never forget that experience – or the influence Chaplin would exert over him, although their styles would be so different.

But what if he had not chosen showbusiness? Considering the extensive brain power that the adult Bob (we'll explain that later) Hope was going to exhibit, the mind boggles as to what he could have achieved with an education. He could have learned himself out of billions.

It wouldn't have been difficult to forecast that the young Hope was going to be a handful. At the age of eight he and a couple of tearaways from his neck of the Cleveland woods broke into a sports store and walked away with a tennis racket and a collection of balls which they proceeded to volley over the nearest high wall – before they themselves were volleyed into a police cell.

It would be nice to think that this experience led to the pugnacious Bob Hope, the one that people would get to know. It's hardly likely, although it did lead him into the boxing ring – 'the only boxer who was actually carried *into* the ring', as he would later say.

For the first time, Leslie Townes Hope changed his name – to Packie East. A friend had gone into the ring with somewhat better results as Packie West. Mr West, or whatever was *his* real name, never had to joke that he was the only boxer in Cleveland who had to wear a rear-view mirror. As for Packie East, he would say he had about four fights before deciding to go into some other business. That was one of his first good decisions. He had a certain instinct about protecting what he would later call his 'ski-slope nose'.

And that was how he got into vaudeville. The nose wasn't instantly visible – not with Leslie Townes Hope, the blackface dancer and comedian. Everyone, or nearly everyone, did blackface in those days. Even some dark-skinned performers who were judged not to be quite dark enough. Leslie did all the usual vaudeville things, like getting jobs wherever he could find them in whatever part of the sticks needed a fill-in act. It meant sitting at the wrong end of the table in vaudeville digs, getting the soup when it was cold, the gristle from the meat when the best parts were all gone, and sleeping in the most uncomfortable room in the house – which he always had to share with one other showbiz hopeful or other.

At five o'clock on the first morning, he'd be lining up with the other down-the-bill performers, ready to offer his music to the orchestra leader before the man became too bored to bother with them.

Hope was a good-looking young man, polished even then, and learned more than showbiz while working in the best nursery the entertainment world ever had. Fred Astaire once told me, 'The trouble with today's entertainers is that they have nowhere to be bad in any more.' Hope learned to be bad – and to be better. He learned, too, enough about the opposite sex to make an evening with a chorus

BOB HOPE

Hope in his twenties, earning $50 a week in vaudeville.

girl more than a mere theatrical experience.

Quite suddenly the lovemaking prowess of Mr Leslie Townes Hope was the talk of the vaudeville circuit. Except that he wasn't Mr Leslie Townes Hope now. He wanted a name that sounded more manly – and looked better on a vaudeville bill.

He had turned himself into *Bob* Hope.

Did Bob find his blackface act insulting to the people who are now called Afro-Americans? He'd be unusual if he did. It was a showbiz convention of the time, made into a fine art by Al Jolson, who always made the black servant the winner in his stage fights with the wicked white plantation owner.

But winning fights was not always at the top of Hope's agenda, hence his interest in the ladies of the profession. One night, Bob found he was spending a little too long being taught the rudiments of certain chorus-line techniques. He rushed panting – if only partly from running the last few yards – through the stage door and had to rush on to his place behind the footlights without the burnt-cork make-up.

'People still laughed,' he said. Somehow, too, his dancing still looked good. So at this point we might pose a further question – another what-if. What if Hope had carried on as a dancer and left the comedy behind – instead of vice versa? He was having to write his own comedy routines – his own jokes in other words. He would say he found it easy enough to be funny and it is true that people did still laugh.

Sometimes, he hit it big. At the town of South Bend, he recalled, he walked out on stage wearing a brown derby hat 'and a cigar stuck in my kisser'. The place erupted with cheers. When he told his first joke, they screamed. Only later did he realize that this was a Catholic audience at a time when the Catholic Al Smith was running for the Presidency and the brown hat and the cigar were his trademark. Later, he faced the same audience but 'didn't get a titter'. By then, Al Smith had lost the election to Herbert Hoover and Hope in the brown hat wasn't funny any more.

But if he *hadn't* concentrated on comedy. . . ? That's the real speculation, but with the benefit of 20-20 hindsight we might hazard a guess: probably, he would have stayed low down the vaudeville bills, dreaming of but never quite becoming a second Astaire.

He struggled and worked with partners, which was either an insurance policy or a cry for help. He was the kind of performer who revelled in attention for himself and only himself. But having a partner enabled them to share the flak as well as the income – and, if things didn't work out, he could always blame the other person. In his case, the other person was George Byrne, with whom he danced and tried out a few comedy routines, sometimes reverting to blackface, too.

They got a few bookings, but not enough. Then came what looked like the big break – an opening in a Broadway show, *The Sidewalks of New York*.

For Bob Hope sidewalks were definitely not paved with gold. The show closed and Hope and Byrne split up. Bob had been turned into a straight man and didn't like it. So he was forced to go back on the road – as a single act.

He enjoyed telling his own jokes by himself. And for a time, audiences seemed to like them, too. But, as in all good showbiz stories, once the show closed, work wasn't as forthcoming as he would have wished – although there were always the occasional bright moments.

He was booked into a revue at New York's Capitol theatre, *Ballyhoo of 1932*. *Ballyhoo* didn't exactly set the Hudson River on fire and was off after four months. But it did contain one element that would prove significant in Hope's life. Also on the bill was a young man who had been singing with the Paul Whiteman Orchestra, a fellow who called himself Bing Crosby. No one had ever been named Bing before and Hope was fascinated by him. Occasionally, they even did an act together – until Crosby went to Hollywood to star in *The Big Broadcast*, a title that would come to have a certain significance in Bob's career, too.

It was already clear, however, that Hope had an intelligence not always obvious in talented performers. The last thing he wanted to do was have a permanent partner. At least publicly and in front of the footlights. Privately? That was a different matter entirely. Offstage, being on his own was certainly the last thought on his mind. He would probably have married quite a few times, for that was the way in those days – if you wanted to make your name in showbiz and still have an active sex life, you married the women in the business.

That was how he came to wed a certain Grace Louis Troxell, whom he had met in his agent's office, taken to his heart and then to his bed. Before that, they had lived together in Bob's apartment, long enough for her to persuade him to include her in his stage act. It was a new act, on the Keith Orpheum Western vaudeville circuit, mainly without dancing. She became the foil of an ever-suffering Mr Hope in the way that another Grace, Gracie Allen, the dumbest of all brilliant dumb blondes, helped George Burns to make Burns and Allen a national institution – that too, was on vaudeville, before graduating to radio and then TV. Hope and Troxell weren't nearly as successful, until, that is, Bob hit on a new formula. He would joke about things in the news. Suddenly, he had found his feet – and Grace's, too. When Bob made people laugh joking about the Depression – 'At least the street cleaners are busy: have you seen the paper thrown out of the skyscrapers?' – he had found his mark. A mark worth $450 a week, slightly different from the $25 he and Grace *had* been earning. Suddenly, they were richer than any member of either of their families had ever been, while the rest of the country was getting poorer. And it wasn't just money: there was prestige, too. The pair were booked into America's greatest vaudeville theatre, the Palace. It was Judy Garland who sang about that house, as they liked to call it in the trade (and Hope would have agreed), 'If you haven't played the Palace, you haven't lived.'

But what was Grace there for? Sure, she could say silly things and make audiences laugh, but while Bob appeared to be the ever-suffering intelligent half, she was losing her value on stage. As far as he was concerned, while they made a hell of a living, it was the *loving* she offered that really occupied Bob's attentions. Then on 25 January 1933, they were married by a justice of the peace at Erie, Pennsylvania. As Hope's biographer Arthur Marx told me, 'I think they went to Erie because you could get married in one day there and it probably took three days in New York and they were likely to be in a hurry. There was never any legal reason for it.'

Years later, Bob would deny emphatically that the marriage ever took place. He said he just took out the licence – a licence clearly available for the public to examine in Erie and one that says that the ceremony took place. Unless there was another couple in Erie at the same time with exactly the same names who not only took out a licence but actually put it into practice, the evidence is overwhelming.

It is also true that, just thirteen months later, Bob married Dolores Reade – in New York. The reason that Bob has always claimed that he never married Grace at any time and that his marriage to Dolores was the one that took place in Erie is subject to a certain degree of speculation. The Erie authorities have no record of a 'second' marriage at all. There must have been a divorce between those two dates. Or *were* those the dates? In July 1934, Bob and Grace were still on the same bill together. Did they work as a pair *after* their marriage folded? Or have the dates become mangled again? Once more, one can only speculate.

With Dolores in 1939. Their marriage looked so good.

It is clear, though, that, when Bob was offered $600 a week to appear at the Capitol Theater, neither a Miss Grace Troxell nor a Mrs Grace Hope was mentioned in the contract. What is also true is that, soon after, Grace married someone else and then had a daughter. Arthur Marx claims that the woman, the product of that second marriage, has regularly received money from Bob's family.

Before Bob and Dolores met in New York, the Hope career was beginning to shine, even without Grace around. Critics were noticing him and, the more they noticed, the more they liked, and the more sophisticated he was becoming.

This was a Bob Hope who began to tell jokes as though they were fired by a machine gun. He knew what was right for him. It was easier to remember one-liners. It was simpler just to deliver a couple of sentences and wait for the laughs. Somehow, he didn't have to wait very long. When he said, 'Long dresses don't bother me, I've got a long memory', the people out front roared.

What was particularly interesting was that they laughed at that in a big, splashy Broadway show. It was called *Roberta*. ⓑ

Chapter Three – ROBERTA

Roberta was the making of Bob Hope, at least the Bob Hope that the world came to know and take to its heart. He played a bandleader who talked even faster than he wielded his baton. It was *the* male part in a show that also featured a certain Sydney Greenstreet as well as Imogene Coca, Fred MacMurray and George Murphy (who after dancing and acting in Hollywood movies became a United States senator) and it had Gene Krupa playing drums down in the pit. But it soon became obvious that the really important role was that of the friend of a football player, of all people, who had inherited a Paris couture house from his Aunt Roberta. And that friend was played by Bob Hope.

It was important in more ways than were anything like apparent at the time, more vital to him than merely being able to offer Dolores the prestige of having a big Broadway star on her arm. It has gone down as one of the significant shows of the 1930s. It boasted a score by Jerome Kern, which was never to be sneezed at, but now particularly because it contained two of his great classic numbers, 'Yesterday' and 'Smoke Gets In Your Eyes'. The music was marvellous, but Hope turned a turgid book into a show that caused more excitement than anything since Fred Astaire and his sister Adele's last thunderous opening night.

He did it with all the cheek and chutzpah (not a word much used in Cleveland, Ohio, and even less in Eltham) that would later be as important a Hope characteristic as his individual style of telling jokes. The show opened in Philadelphia to the kinds of review that send many people in the world of entertainment to either their nearest psychiatrist's couch or to the poison cupboard. They weren't merely disappointing, they were terrible. If the name Jerome Kern hadn't been attached to them, they would have been catastrophic. *Gowns By Roberta*, the show was called then. An immediate decision was taken to lose the first two words. It was due to Bob Hope that other words were actually *added* to the show. And it is there that the true significance of *Roberta* to Hope's career becomes clear.

It was Bob who suggested that a joke or two could brighten up the whole piece. Kern agreed. Otto Harbach, his lyricist, did not. But Kern and Hope won out – and so did the show. It was Bob himself who inserted the lines that made all the difference, even if the critics thought he was trying to be too clever by half.

The verse to the 'Smoke Gets In Your Eyes' number began with the words, 'There's an old Russian proverb, "When your heart's on fire, smoke gets in your eyes".' Hope interjected at that point the devastatingly funny line, 'We have a

Bob in 1938. The trappings of wealth came quickly.

Good-looking and smart (in both senses of the word).

proverb in America, too. Love is like hash. You have to have confidence in it to enjoy it.' Well, in 1933 that was considered funny, which gives one some idea how ideas of humour have changed in the last six or seven decades.

It wasn't just that Hope line that made the difference, but others that came and went in the nine months that *Roberta* ran at Broadway's New Amsterdam Theater. In the midst of the action, or what served as action, he would turn to the audience like Groucho in a Marx Brothers film with a joke that had absolutely nothing to do with the plot. That in itself wasn't significant. What was important was that Bob bought the lines from a professional joke writer named Billy Reade. Every time he used one, he paid anything from $5 to $10 for it (but sometimes 'forgot' to pay anything).

They weren't particularly good jokes and the practice didn't last very long since Harbach protested at the way the interjections were ruining the poetry of his lyrics, but they showed an art that Bob Hope was honing for himself. Not only could he make people laugh with his own stories, he could also turn the words crafted by others into material that seemed to have been created there and then, on the spur of the moment, by Bob himself. It was the beginning of the joke factory. Such is the development of a star and a star act.

Roberta ended its run and became part of that Broadway canon. Before long, the show would turn into a Hollywood film starring Fred Astaire (no one yet thought that Bob Hope was a big enough name to carry a movie that would be sold all round the world). Years later, Bob himself would reprise the role twice on American television, a demonstration of either his perennial youth or of the increasingly frequent inability in his later years to judge what was right for him and what was wrong.

But in 1934 those years were far off. He was developing a mind that was as sharp for the next career opportunity as it was for the right joke to suit his style. He did everything that an up-and-coming star would expect to do, not excluding the odd return to vaudeville (and, as we have seen, a return with Grace Louise).

There was, for instance, radio – and in the early 1930s this burgeoning medium was showing signs of being the biggest thing that show business had ever known. But few people really knew how to handle it. Hope, though, was taking it seriously and because he took it seriously wanted to do something different. That was how his 'song sketch' idea took off – doing a comical playlet around a song.

Every star who was any star at all was being enticed on to the airwaves – and, in truth, most of them didn't need any enticing. Nightclubs that had 'wires' – links with radio stations – would promote their bands and singing stars by being able to put them on the air every night of the week. But what Bob Hope was doing now was much bigger than that. He was appearing on shows like *The Fleischmann Yeast Hour,* starring Rudy Vallee, who was a top crooner even before Bing Crosby was known as the Groaner.

Vallee would say later that he never remembered Bob's appearances on his show – comedians were never more than fill-ins. Walter Scharf, who was musical director of the programme, told me, too, that he had no recollection of Hope appearing. 'But I remember conducting the band at a couple of nightclubs in Chicago when he and Dolores appeared together. He was a very difficult man to those who worked with him, always wanting his own way and not being terribly nice to Dolores either.'

It was in Chicago that Bob rejected one of the first suggestions that have been made to him in the course of his career. A theatre manager suggested that he might like to appear on stage solely as a singer. 'I don't know what that said about my comedy,' he would joke, 'but I liked the gags pretty much.'

If nothing else, this short episode provides us with another opportunity to wonder what might have been. Meanwhile, Dolores was continuing to sing at fashionable New York nighteries. She enjoyed singing and did it well. 'Have You Ever Seen A Dream Walkin?' brought the house down wherever she sang it, but what she really wanted to do was to have children. Not long into her marriage, she discovered this was not going to be possible.

If this worried Bob, he gave little outward sign of it. He was offered $5,000 a time to make films at the Astoria studios in New York, the place where the Marx

BOB HOPE

Brothers and every other star who didn't fancy making the trip to California worked and where Woody Allen has been filming in more recent years.

Going Spanish was not the boost to his career that *Roberta* had been. 'I wanted to run, not walk, to the nearest fire exit,' he said at the time. The film itself wasn't noticed by the critics, but the Hope comment was – and Educational Films, who had put him under contract, immediately cancelled the agreement. But, then, Bob Hope and movies weren't made for each other, were they?

He knew there were other things in the offing and, if he was going to show any real interest in them, they had to be good. A man who could command $5,000 a week knew his value, even when ostensibly he was out of work. For four months he starred in a light-hearted musical comedy (the more sophisticated 'musical' was almost a decade away) called *Say When*. But, when the audiences said when, it was time to look for other things. There were always offers on the table and he was in a position to choose what he wanted. What was more, he was demanding that Dolores should work with him.

So when the notion of appearing for the Loew's chain of theatres – cinemas that had top-class vaudeville turns, too – was put to him, he accepted on behalf of his wife and himself. It might just be a holding operation, but both were willing to hold on with a salary that many another performer would have been happy to accept for life.

It was then that Hope decided that he needed lines that could fill his entire routine – lines written by other people. He looked around for the talent who would feed his needs – but not cost him too much. And that was how Melville Shavelson entered his life.

Shavelson would soon become one of Hope's top writers. It didn't look as if he would end up that way when they first met – Bob had employed Al Boasberg, one of the great wits of his time but who was now looking for new talent; Boasberg was probably getting expensive. Shavelson was working for a New York publicist named Milt Josefsberg for $15 a week, which was two dollars more than he had been earning the week before. It was Josefsberg who had told him about Bob Hope, the coming star attraction at Loew's State Theater. More important to them was the fact that this Mr Hope had been booked for a new radio series, *The Woodbury Soap Show*.

Until then, radio was just something in which Bob was usually billed after the words, 'Also taking part were. . . ' He had one other writer, but even to do that, to invest part of his own salary in another man, showed a degree of prescience. That one writer, Wilkie Mahoney, who was best known in the business as the editor of *Uncle Billy's Whiz Bang*, provided him with enough material for five minutes a week on programmes like *The Lucky Strike Hit Parade*. Now that was not going to be enough.

Before, radio had never excited Bob all that much. The money was just so-so and the exposure was limited to the odd line he managed to sandwich in between the commercials for Bromo Seltzer. This was going to be different. As he told Mel Shavelson for his book *Don't Shoot, It's Only Me*, 'the radio season lasted thirty-nine weeks. That meant I had to tell thirty-nine times as many jokes as I had used in a whole year of vaudeville. Talented though I was, I knew I couldn't steal that many jokes in one year.'

He was about to enter a new world, where he couldn't tell the same joke night after night and still be rewarded with audiences and laughter. Radio, like television a generation later, swallowed material like a hungry shark, and that was why employing writers was not just a good idea. It was vital.

Hope once said, 'There's a lot of truth in that. Anyone who does all the things I do has got to have a large staff. When you get into a business like I have with radio, television and pictures you've got to have an awfully good staff.'

Shavelson and Josefsberg were going to be the nucleus of that awfully good staff, even if they didn't realize it the day they were received into Bob Hope's suite at the Hampshire House hotel, overlooking Central Park, the kind of establishment lowly PR people entered only on behalf of other people. This time they were representing themselves – and were presenting the great man (as he liked to consider himself) with a script they had spent a day writing.

'How much do you guys expect to be paid for writing this crap?' was the kind response from a comedian eyeing lines that could enhance his reputation but not wanting to admit it.

Josefsberg, who had been appointed spokesman for the pair ('He outweighed me by a hundred pounds,' said Shavelson, 'most of it ketchup, to which he was addicted') came up with the answer: 'We usually get a hundred dollars a week.'

'Each?' asked Hope.

'Each,' said the optimistic writer, who, as Shavelson pointed out, always had another business to fall back on.

Shavelson says he almost fainted – and so did Hope, who could only reply, 'That's a little rich for my blood.'

The stage directions for what happened next were predictable to the young Shavelson, then barely twenty years old. As he told me, 'I almost fainted. Nobody in my family had ever been paid a hundred dollars for anything unless they had faked an injury on their insurance policy. I wanted to dissolve our partnership immediately, on the grounds of temporary insanity.'

Josefsberg, however, knew his quarry. In the elevator going down to the ground, he reassured his partner. 'Don't worry,' he said, 'we'll get it. That comedian couldn't think of anything funny to say. He needs us.'

Hope seemed to agree. 'After three weeks struggling against his better judgement, we got the money and a contract,' Mel told me. 'Under its terms, I think I am still obligated to deliver a monologue joke whenever he calls.'

The jokers were ready with the jokes, ready for the start of what would be a nationally networked show. They were also let into the secret of the song sketch, which had been in Bob's mind but now was going to be used for the first time. The first one was called 'Ride Tenderfoot Ride' – 'which thankfully has disappeared'. Nevertheless, it served as a good lesson to both the writers and the star. Bob turned up in the radio studio wearing a ten-gallon hat and carrying pistols. 'The audience was confused and so were we,' says Shavelson. 'What was he doing wearing costume for a radio show?' He never did it again.

Shavelson had no difficulty in assessing his boss's talent. Why, I asked him, if he depended on writers to provide him with so much stuff, couldn't the writers simply tell the jokes themselves? 'That is the mystery of Bob Hope,' he told me. 'If we *could* all do it, we'd all be as successful and as charming as Bob Hope.'

Hope was about to be successful and charming on another Broadway stage, one that interested him much, much more than seeing 'my nose being stretched over that big screen'.

The new offer was to enter the portals over which had been inscribed the legend that there had walked the most beautiful women in the world, the Ziegfeld Girls. He was invited to be featured in the latest *Ziegfeld Follies*, a title that had few rivals on Broadway, two words that meant the most lavish productions ever seen on a stage. Florenz Ziegfeld himself had always insisted that every inch of stitching on his girls' gowns be done by hand – not that anyone else could see it, but because he himself knew that they were the best. His stars had the same degree of perfection about them – Eddie Cantor and Will Rogers, Fanny Brice and Sophie Tucker. And now Bob Hope.

Ziegfeld himself had been dead for four years and the show was now in the hands of the Shubert brothers, the men who had brought Jolson and countless other performers to Broadway for the first time. Hope did not disappoint them any more than he would have disappointed Florenz Ziegfeld – and he was not disappointed with himself, either. The men who treated their stars rather as a farmer treats a prize bull – with reluctant respect – recognized that they had in Bob just the man to please their audiences. It had all the right packaging, as Hope knew it would. Josephine Baker was one of his co-stars; the director and designer was Vincente Minnelli. Vernon Duke provided the music and Ira Gershwin wrote the lyrics. It was Bob who had been handed the 'star' song, 'I Can't Get Started'.

Now that, too, was a revelation. Bob Hope, former boxer turned dancer who wanted to be known as a comedian, was seen and heard to have a very nice singing voice. Very nice indeed. It was a high voice, not a great one. But, as he would later prove, he could sing well enough for that voice to be heard on gramophone records that spun on turntables at 78r.p.m.

And there we have precisely what was different about Bob Hope. At barely thirty, he was proving he was an all-round entertainer, which was precisely what

*With his brother Jack
and (centre) Jack Benny.*

the people clamouring for tickets for Broadway shows – to say nothing of the producers of those shows – wanted. There were plenty of other performers who made people laugh, and the record stores were bursting with those heavy, scratchy discs made by singers who could warble a tune – and only Fred Astaire was really able to sing as well as dance. But when Fred told jokes, he even embarrassed himself. Bob was never to be embarrassed by anything. Singer, dancer, comedian. He was all those things.

'I think Hope was a very good singer,' the writer and director Hal Kanter explained to me, 'if not a singer whom musicians could appreciate. But the songwriters could appreciate him because he could sell a song.'

More important than anything else about him, he was good in all the things he did. He probably would never have been an Astaire, good enough to dance on the stage without doing anything else, but nobody laughed when he moved and more often than not they applauded. The singing voice was not as strong as that of Jolson or Crosby, but plenty of young men who revelled in the job description 'crooner' wouldn't have been unhappy with the pipes he had been given and the way he used them. As for his jokes, he was beginning to sound different from anyone else. His fellow Ziegfeld artist, Will Rogers was still best known for telling topical stories, but he did it his own way – a slow languid way while he dressed in

Western gear and twirled a rope. Even when he played a part in a movie, he still gave out the kind of easygoing homespun philosophy that customers for his Broadway shows had come to expect.

With Bob Hope there was no philosophy – save perhaps the most important of all: that of making people laugh and getting paid extraordinarily well for doing so. He learned his material and was able to perform it better every time. Which led to another discovery: Bob Hope was becoming a very capable actor.

He was also not just exceedingly successful as a funny dancing, singing man, but he was charming, too. That's what audiences of the *Follies* demanded. The women came to the theatre in glittering gowns that had the fashion photographers drooling. They shimmered in on the arms of men immaculate in tail coats over stiff white shirts who carried top hats.

They liked him, but it wasn't all that he wanted. The Bob Hope of 1936 was a man with enough ambition to power a steam engine, which in many ways was precisely what he was: a speeding engine that thundered from one line to the next. At the *Follies* audiences saw for the first time the Hope who, before long, would be a national institution.

But he wasn't entirely happy there. He needed more than being sandwiched between those beautiful girls – especially since Dolores was too close for comfort. These were very early days in their marriage and she wasn't about to let him get too close to those tall girls who showed perhaps just a little too much leg and certainly too much bosom for her pleasure. She watched him like a schoolteacher making sure that the little boys didn't put a white mouse in the girls' desks. Faced with the competition of the more leggy, busty and sexy Ziegfeld girls, Dolores saw her Bob as a much more risky character than any little mouse.

Hope wanted to be able to shine as an actor – as well as a comedian and singer. There was every chance to do all three in the new Broadway show, *Red, Hot and Blue*, which was also going to star Ethel Merman and Jimmy Durante. Actually, they were the *real* stars and neither of them would agree on very much, except that Bob was going to be third. Both wanted to have their names listed first on programmes and posters. Cole Porter, who wrote the score and virtually produced the show, came up with the answer: they would be criss-crossed, so that neither of them would be seen to be first – and, to make things even fairer, their positions would be changed every fortnight. It has come to be one of the great stories in Broadway history. Bob's success in the show was another.

He told jokes – again, jokes he didn't write himself – and he sang songs. The best of those was the Porter standard, 'It's De-Lovely'. It wouldn't be true to say that the standard is now remembered for Bob's version alone. But he was the first to sing a tune that is always included in any Cole Porter songbook. It was also to be featured on the first record that had the name Bob Hope on the label.

The show lasted less than four months, but they were four months that were

Bob and Bing. The partnership went on and on and on...

going to be important in the life of Bob Hope.

The new tune, of course, had more than one airing on *The Woodbury Soap Show*. It seemed that Bob's career was now set. Here was a Broadway star who was constantly being offered new scripts of new productions who was one of the most popular names on radio. Had he any doubts about that popularity, Bing Crosby was ready to put those doubts out of his mind. If imitation is the sincerest form of flattery, friendly mockery runs a close second. Virtually every week, Bing, on his own *Kraft Music Hall* radio programme, insulted Bob and Bob's nose while Hope got his own back by commenting on Crosby and the ever-increasing Crosby waistline. It was the real beginning of the Bing and Bob feud that would prove such a crowd-puller.

There were now going to be many more opportunities for such banter. In 1937, Paramount Pictures were planning a new film that combined movies with the world that Bob Hope had by now taken to be his own: radio. They were going to call it *The Big Broadcast of 1938*. 'We'd like you to be in it,' said the studio. 'We'd like to come,' said Dolores. Bob Hope was on the way to Hollywood. 🅑🅗

Chapter Four – THE ROAD TO HOLLYWOOD

Bob Hope went to California with $100,000 in a briefcase, which gives some idea of the kind of success he had been in the past couple of years and of his attitude to money. According to Bob Slatzer, who later worked for him as a publicist, that was because he did not trust banks.

He didn't like railway trains either. He travelled west by road – sharing the driving with his brother George in an old Packard sports car.

They arrived in Nebraska in the middle of a snowstorm. The blizzard was at its worst when Bob crashed the car. He had slammed on the brakes, but the car skidded and smashed into a stationary truck. George held his hands in front of his brother's face so that they would take the force of the collision. The crashing glass splinters lacerated George's hands and he bore the scars for ever afterwards. Bob caught a sliver of glass close to his lip – and that scar could be spotted in screen close-ups, but without George it would have been much worse. He never forgot his brother's help and he gave him work for the rest of his life.

The Big Broadcast of 1938 was the Big Break for Bob Hope. It could also have been the big break for that ski-slope nose of his. The studio wanted it changed. Dolores said no and the Bob Hope career in pictures was launched down that very slope.

No matter how successful he had become on Broadway, it was a very limited elite market. However popular *The Woodbury Soap Show* had been – it was not at all today's idea of a soap opera – it was for a limited season and was never going to be heard outside the United States. Now, Bob was about to become an international star.

There had been *Big Broadcast* movies ever since Bing Crosby joined the Mills Brothers and the man who rejoiced in the title the Street Singer, Arthur Tracy, in the first of the series in 1932. It was followed by *Big Broadcasts* of 1935 and 1937 before Bob Hope's big-time movie debut in the 1938 version.

It is difficult to reason why anyone should want to put a year to any movie. The very identification with a particular year would seem to date it in more ways than one, but, in this case, it was seen as a reasonable way of cashing in on a successful formula. Broadcasting was, after all, the most popular entertainment medium of the age.

The story – about the problems of a steamship owner involved in an international race – didn't matter in the slightest. What did matter was the song Bob sang to one of his numerous co-stars, Shirley Ross. The song, written by

The Big Broadcast of 1938

Ralph Rainger and Leo Robin, was to be the most important in Hope's life – 'Thanks For the Memory'. No one could have known it would turn out as more than a simple melody performed by a once-married couple recalling the nicer things that happened when they were together – not unlike the memories of Noël Coward and Gertrude Lawrence. No one could have predicted it would have become even more important to him than 'Pennies From Heaven' would be to Crosby. Bing would always sing the same lyrics to *his* song, but Hope would have new words for his at every gig he played. It would serve not merely as a signature tune but as a valedictory hymn to the people to whom he was performing. There would always be new words for each hospital, army camp or charity audience.

'I had no idea it would be played more often than "The Star-Spangled Banner",' says Mel Shavelson today. Years ago, Leo Robin told me, 'It was one of those silly moments of inspiration, I suppose you'd call it. I was told the rough plot line and came up with it.'

At best he might have thought it would be an updated setting for the kind of thing that Coward wrote in *Private Lives*, the couple who unexpectedly meet again and realize that they hadn't left everything they liked about each other behind in the divorce court. Hope would later have reason to be grateful for that moment of inspiration.

As Shavelson told me, 'The song has become a joke because of being repeated so many times, but it was done quite seriously, even though it's an amusing song in the picture. It was a combination of the romance on board the ship between Bob and Shirley Ross and, if you listen to the lyrics, they're very good, very clever and they have a lot of sentiment about them – and Bob put it all over legitimately, a legitimate song with a lot of fun.'

It wasn't, however, to be the only notable thing that happened in the film. There was that bevy of co-stars – including, not just Ross, but also W.C. Fields, Martha Ray, Lynn Overman and a certain lady who would herself become quite an important memory for which Bob Hope would have cause to give thanks – a lady by the name of Dorothy Lamour.

They had met first when Bob was in New York. In those days, he and Dolores would call in after their shows at whatever ex-speakeasy was in vogue at the time, have a drink (which was still a novel thing to be able to do legally) and listen to the cabaret. In a couple of the places, notably one rejoicing in the name One Fifth Avenue, Dorothy, then a young sultry brunette, provided the entertainment.

He couldn't have known then how important she would be in his career, although Dolores probably worried that she might be rather more important than she would have liked. There is no evidence that the Hope–Lamour relationship was anything other than completely professional. Besides, it was Shirley Ross (today remembered – if at all – solely for her Hope duets) who was the co-star in this new film. She and Hope went to a nightclub one night and Bob was invited to

On board in the movie which made Bob big: The Big Broadcast of 1938.

perform. When he was introduced by the *Big Broadcast* director Mitchell Leisen as 'Bob *Hoke*', it was not only unflattering to the kind of humour he was offering, but said a lot for his fame on the West Coast. When they clapped politely, nobody seemed any the wiser.

Certainly, other women were left in no doubt who this up-and-coming star was and where his great talents lay. They had to be impressed. Everywhere he went, except in those more intimate moments when he was interested only in the company of one person at a time, there was now an entourage – his agent 'Doctor' Louis Shurr, his director and at least one of his writers.

Mel Shavelson had been employed by Hope to work with him on the *Woodbury Soap Show*, which still went out from New York, but with Bob providing his own input from studios in Los Angeles. Shavelson wasn't the only one supplying the cracks that distinguished Hope from the other comedians, the ones who looked around for the clever writer who could come up with the right situation to fit the right story. Bob already was the proprietor of a maturing joke factory, not yet in full mass production, but turning out prototype gags for all the stories that would follow.

It wasn't just the writers who were needed. There was another magic ingredient that had eluded him on the first broadcast that he performed live from California – an audience. He knew he needed people out front off whom he could bounce his writers' stories. NBC had thought he could just tell his gags along their coast-to-coast line and everyone would laugh. So a scratch audience, left over from another programme, was found and he got most of the laughs he wanted. The following week, the network gave away tickets for the show and people told him they fell off their seats both in the studio and listening to him on those big bulky radio sets that defined the age.

They plainly also defined Bob Hope's comedy and the control he had over it. He knew – and right into old age always would know – what he needed to make things work exactly for *him*. And, apparently, not just what worked in front of an audience of millions.

His writers were there now to plan a new radio series – *The Pepsodent Show*. The programme was to make Hope's name as synonymous with toothpaste as toothpaste was with his name. Before long, people would walk into drugstores and ask for a tube of Bob Hope, and they weren't being funny. (If they were, he would have hired them as writers.) To the professional writers, it was a great opportunity, a golden opportunity, to get in on what was fast becoming, as Shavelson put it, 'the golden age of comedy – most of the gold being his'.

It was also becoming the golden age of Bob Hope films, although two quickie follow-ups to *The Big Broadcast* – *College Swing* and *Give Me A Sailor* – gave little indication that anything important was about to happen. When Paramount decided to make fuller use of the contract that they had signed with Bob at precisely the time the radio network were talking about *The Pepsodent Show*, Hope knew he had to bring in the best writers available, which was how Mel Shavelson and his more sophisticated partner Milt Josefsberg were sent the train fare to go to Hollywood.

The idea of writing for Hope appealed to them. He wasn't like other comedians of the day. They themselves were young, enthusiastic and had the sort of wit that he had. They were tempted by the thought of writing for a man who regarded jokes as important commodities – and, like the best gifts that come in small packages, gags that were short and pithy.

Now they were being offered the chance of a lifetime. They were not just pleased to get the fare, but were thrilled to be waved past the guards at the Paramount lot and shown into the great young man's dressing room, the kind that befitted a person of his status. When the status increased still further, so did the dressing room and what Bob would do in it. For the moment, however, he was more than content with managing a career that seemed to rename him Bob 'Prospects' Hope. His fourth Paramount film was going to be a much more vital vehicle and one that would have his name emblazoned all over the publicity material. *Thanks For The Memory* was plainly intended to cash in on the success of the song with the same name. It also co-starred Shirley Ross. Leo Robin and Ralph Rainger provided another song which this time everyone said would not just be more successful than 'The Star-Spangled Banner' but would take the shine off 'God Save The King', too. They weren't quite right, although 'Two Sleepy People' (which cribbed the words 'dawn's early light' from the American National Anthem, just to underline its superiority) did enjoy phenomenal popularity.

That was the climate in which the two writers were welcomed by their boss. Shavelson, however, wasn't there merely to write. As far as Hope was concerned, he had an additional value – even though the star showed concern that the two men had been in Hollywood for a whole morning without writing a line for him. Shavelson explained that, guiltily, he had spent the morning hunting for an apartment and had found one in what was the medium-rent district of Fountain Avenue. That interested Hope more than might have seemed reasonable for a man at the top of his career and in costume and make-up for his exciting new movie role.

'Are you married?' he asked his writer. Shavelson said that no, he wasn't. 'No one to share your apartment with?' As Mel says now, he wondered if he wanted to move in with him, but he knew Bob had a rented home in the San Fernando Valley and 'an unrentable wife'. He didn't realize there and then that the unrentable wife was going to be the real problem with his boss. After singing 'Two Sleepy People' to his two sleepy writers and asking for their opinion – as if they could have said anything bad about it – he happened to suggest that Shavelson could do worse than leave the keys to his apartment behind on his way out. Mel knew on which side his contract was buttered and said he would do just that – and hoped that the great star wouldn't mind leaving them in the mail box when he had finished with them. At about midnight.

Why he wanted the keys Shavelson didn't really know. The writer didn't realize until it was explained to him that Hope could find a use for an unoccupied flat and one that *Mrs* Hope would not totally approve of. He also didn't realize that that would be a good plot for a movie script. Had he done so, he could have beaten Billy Wilder to an Oscar-winning idea. Whether Jack Lemmon ever realized that, when he made *The Apartment*, he was playing the part of Mel Shavelson, is not on the record. But the memory of what Mel describes as the 'still-warm key' left for him in his mail box and the equally warm sheets remains pretty vivid. So is the memory of two sets of wet footsteps leading from the shower room to the bed.

Bob Hope's practice for pay day is equally illustrative of the man's quirky humour. Other stars found demeaning ways of paying their underlings – accountants counting out the dollar bills in front of people who had no right to see such things, secretaries doling out cheques as though they were doing some extraordinary favour. Hope had as much of his own endearing and totally original style in paying people as he did in reciting their lines. He would stand at the top of a staircase next to the office in his Valley home and make paper aeroplanes of the cheques. Then he would proceed to fly the planes down to the 'greedy' writers – like a bird offering a worm to the gaping beaks of her young. Somehow there wasn't quite the same spirit of affection in Bob's intentions. The writers ran for their cheques and showed their appreciation of the man who said it was the only exercise the lazy sons of bitches ever got.

As Mel Shavelson told me, 'We all felt that writing for Hope had nothing to do with earning a living – at least, our living. Yes, he did have a way of holding on to a

BOB HOPE

nickel quite well. He owes me quite a bit of money for newspapers and other things I bought for him.'

Yet he is the first to admit why that practice of the flying cheques came to an end. 'The cheques got so big, you couldn't fly them any more.' Not only that, he also gave presents. 'I've got gold cufflinks from him – nothing very expensive,' says Mel. 'I've got lots of presents. He said he appreciated us, but not very often.'

There was one experience when the Hope team were in Atlanta on tour that said a lot (or a little) for Bob's monetary husbandry. The eighty-year-old father of another writer, Norman Sullivan, had joined the party for a breakfast at which Bob entertained the throng. Eventually, the bill arrived. Bob stared at it for a long time and then said to Sullivan, 'Norman, you're not going to allow your father to pay for this, are you?'

There were eight of them employed in the factory by now, all of whom were expected to write a whole radio show as if they were the only ones on the job. Hope then made them read their 'shows' out loud. If he laughed, they kept their jobs. If he didn't – and if the other writers didn't – they were out. Bob Hope's way of easing the unemployment statistics of the United States was to take on another five writers, making thirteen altogether, and fire the five who got the fewest laughs. That way he always had eight on the staff. But he was clever. While the hapless five were working out their notice, he still had their talents at his disposal.

Hope has always justified that and has never regretted it. 'I always wanted the writers to read to each other out loud. If you got a good reaction from another writer, you knew it was really funny.'

He held the sword of Damocles over them all. 'The Depression was still with us and you had to eat,' said Shavelson. 'If you could get these guys whose jobs depended upon their *not* laughing to laugh at a joke, then Bob would be satisfied.'

The problem of reading the jokes gave that writer his first ulcer, but soon it was generally accepted as the way to 'play' a gag and even a whole programme. 'After a while it became a sort of a club and both Bob and Sid Caesar found that, by getting a group of writers in a room and letting them kick a topic around, they usually came up with more angles, more fun than they would have from somebody sitting alone and manufacturing it with a typewriter.'

Later, during the actual programme, they would be required to sit in a booth and check the *sort* of laugh their jokes got. A large tick on a sheet of paper they carried with them was great. If there was a line through the tick, it proved to be even greater than that. Superb was a tick with two lines in it. Says Shavelson, 'Amazing how many of his own jokes a writer would give one of those.' Bad joke got a number 1. If they were slightly better, they got a 2 and so on.

That was the pattern and that was how Bob Hope became the most successful radio comedian in history. For the writers, the pressure was terrible. 'It was a revolving door and the writers would come and go.'

34

The question was: Who was he more scared of – the skeleton or Paulette Goddard? In The Cat and the Canary.

Before long, Mel needed his job as much as the others on the team. He was getting married and asked for time off for a honeymoon. 'Take two and a half hours tomorrow afternoon,' said Hope. 'That should be enough.' It was enough for Bob Hope, who expected everyone to dance to his tune, particularly if it was *Thanks for the Memory*. The memory of that half an afternoon's honeymoon is as strong as that of the warm key and the paper aeroplanes.

None of this should be allowed to diminish what was Hope's very genuine talent. Or his appeal. He took his radio show on to the road and at the same time did live gigs at the movie theatres showing *Thanks For The Memory*. Thousands thronged the cinemas for the four shows a day. He himself was on a percentage of the profits and, when he saw how many people were lining up, he ordered that the four shows should be increased to six.

'We can't,' said the theatre owner. 'Your film runs for ninety-four minutes and there won't be time.' Bob's answer was simple: 'Take out two reels and they'll never notice.' Before long, the theatre took out four reels. 'But,' says Mel Shavelson, 'he got mad when he saw people in the front row who had been sitting through two shows and he made them leave the theatre.' He also made his agent ring Paramount and arrange for his fee for the tour to be trebled. That was how Bob Hope did business.

Pepsodent took up his option of a second radio series as avidly as Paramount wanted more movies. The shows, like all American comedy programmes, were essentially variety performances with Bob the star turn. There were sketches and opportunities for the barrage of jokes. Hope liked them more than anything else he did. He didn't have to remember any lines. He could just stand before the microphone and read what his writers had written for him.

That, too, was another of the great Hope talents. He was a great reader, unlike many other performers. Actually, he didn't just read those scripts, he played them as though they were musical instruments. The timing, the breath control, the crescendos just before the laughs came were almost musical experiences.

While Bob Hope's ability to deliver lines straight from the script was a pretty good demonstration of good acting, it did not make him an actor. *The Cat and the Canary*, however, did.

Bob co-starred with Paulette Goddard, soon to be the wife of Charlie Chaplin, in this movie, in which he was not just funny, but played an intelligent part extremely ... well, intelligently.

It would be a characteristic noted in the decades to come. He had to be intelligent to be able to work in the subtleties of the jokes, even if they had been written for him by other people. But sometimes that very intelligence was defeated by his comedy. As Melville Shavelson says, 'You never looked on Bob as a big movie star because he didn't have that big-star aura about him; he was always making fun of it.'

The film set the pattern of Bob Hope's screen persona for ever afterwards. Here he was in the midst of a Louisiana bayou with fog and swamps all around the spooky house where a family gather to hear the will of their newly departed eccentric relative – and he was more scared than anyone sitting in the circle at a movie theatre. As every door creaked and each unexpected corpse appeared, you felt as though he was going to jump out from the screen and into the arms of the woman in the front row. But he still made them laugh. 'Bob Hope can joke, apparently, even with a risen corpse,' said the *Monthly Film Bulletin* approvingly.

Goddard was as beautiful as the studio hoped she would be. Hope was better than anyone *could* have hoped, better at showing that, when it came to being yellow, he had been dropped into a vat of super-quality paint. He was to say that he enjoyed working for the studio that gave him this opportunity. 'Paramount always treated me fairly. As soon as I became a greater draw, they paid me more. All I had to do was ask them for it in a threatening way.' When you saw the baby-chicken-yellow Hope in the movies, he bared his teeth, snarled and then ran for the nearest exit. In real life the Hope threats were a lot more convincing.

His radio shows made him totally persuasive. As *The Cat and the Canary* proved, put his name on a theatre marquee and audiences who tuned into *The Pepsodent Show* every week were ready to put down their money at the box office. The film was so successful, a sequel was instantly organized, also starring Paulette Goddard, called this time *Ghost Breakers*.

This one was set in a West Indian castle (if you could accept that, you could accept anything) and marked, too, the first time that Anthony Quinn had worked with Hope. 'I enjoyed the experience very much,' Quinn told me.

It was to be an experience renewed. Paramount now had the notion that audiences wanted to see more of the Hope they knew from his radio performances. So they offered him a movie in which he could sing songs and move to the sound of one of the best orchestras in Hollywood, and, together with a new partner, he created an institution. A cliché? Maybe. But a lot of other people in show business have created institutions and not just the hospitals and old folks' homes that bear their names. The institution Hope helped create has to rank alongside those Follies of Mr Ziegfeld, the musicals of MGM and that cigar of George Burns.

Here, again, he was scared of his own shadow and always lost the girl at the end of the movie. But this time it was a girl in a sarong, a girl called Dorothy Lamour. And the guy to whom he lost that girl was Bing Crosby. *The Road to Singapore* wasn't the funniest film ever made and nothing like the best of its genre, but it struck a chord with audiences all over the world and began that love affair between Bob Hope and his public that was to last sixty years.

Nobody planned it as the start of a whole new series, a whole new phenomenon. How could they? How do you know that people are going to like more scrambled eggs than enjoy them sunny side up? This *Road* picture was sunny side up all the way and it was clear from the beginning that there would be more to come.

What made it so was the innate chemistry between Crosby and Hope. For most of the time, that chemistry was focused around Lamour, but she was never more than a third party, someone who had to be there for the story's sake. Bob Slatzer, who was a publicist on the *Road* films, explains, 'Bing wouldn't give her the time of day, whereas Bob would always listen to her. I once asked her why she never pushed it more, and she just said there was nothing to push.'

But her problems were not allowed to show on the screen. Not that that story was ever more than incidental to the laughter generated by what was already being spoken of as the best comedy team since Laurel and Hardy. Abbott and Costello, who had recently started their series of wacky comedies, would have had good reason to worry about Bing and Bob, but for one thing: Abbott was lost without Costello. Bing and Bob had no intention of forgoing their own brilliantly successful individual careers for the sake of a partnership that might or might not take off. Also, despite all the nonsense, they were a whole lot more sophisticated than the pair who had the kids lining up outside cinemas on Saturday afternoons.

As in all good stories, this one might never have happened. The studio had had the idea of a movie featuring Fred MacMurray and Jack Oakie and then changed their mind. The script, they thought, would be ideal for George Burns and Gracie Allen. They had a title all ready, *The Road To Mandalay*, itself a remake of a 1926 film, but it never got off the ground. By the time that Paramount got round to

Always competing. Bing and Bob fight over Dorothy Lamour in The Road To Singapore.

making the movie, Burns and Allen were no longer available and the studio heads had to think of taking the project out of its archive, dusting off the script and finding a couple of players under one of their contracts to take over.

They chose the new title only after choosing the new stars – there was a risk that *Mandalay* would make too many people think of the Rudyard Kipling song and this owed nothing to that. The great success of the film, which turned out to be not just the first but also – with one exception – the worst of the series, was due to the inspired idea of teaming Hope and Crosby, using the established crooner as part of a comedy team and allowing the comedian to sing to his heart's content, too. If it took off, it would make both men even bigger stars than they were already and make Paramount a great deal of money.

And the idea of the *Road* films certainly did take off, establishing a whole swathe of conventions on the way – like Bob breaking off from the action to talk to the audience, or the pair sending the villain off to the obscure land of the Paramount contract player – after a sudden and irrelevant game of pat-a-cake.

Audiences liked some films to have ideas that were sudden and irrelevant. They also liked conventions – particularly when they upset every other film's notion of what was and what was not normal.

The fact that it was Crosby who always got the girl was itself funny. Certainly, he had the better voice and was given every chance to use it to the best advantage, but the idea of a beautiful girl preferring him over Hope was ludicrous. Crosby had as much idea of good dress sense as a Boy Scout. Hope was immaculate. Crosby was tubby and wore his hat most of the time so that he could avoid having to use his toupée. Hope was very attractive to women who in real life ran to his bed at the drop of a bra. That was well known in Paramount – so his failure to get the girl was something of an in-joke. There were other in-jokes, too, such as quips about the studio – including the ludicrous spectacle of a Paramount executive wearing a tuxedo walking through the set in the midst of what served as the action, and saying, 'I'm taking a short cut to studio five.'

Dorothy Lamour was essential to the movie. There had to be a love interest and the fact that she wore a sarong established another tradition. 'You know Lamour,' Bob said, 'the girl who started on a shoe string and now wears it for her costume.' Because she looked so good with seemingly no more than a few inches of cotton between her and the indecency laws, she was never going to be allowed to wear much more.

But she wasn't given the star-studded treatment accorded to the two male leads. Neither did she fit in with the buddy-buddy lifestyle of the two men, or at least what appeared to be a buddy-buddy lifestyle. 'It was a question of status,' Anthony Quinn, who went straight from *Ghost Breakers* into *Singapore* with Hope, told me. 'They were always very nice to me, but I never sat at their table. I was much more lowly. I wasn't let into any of their business deals. And I know Dotty Lamour wasn't, either.'

That was to be another intriguing feature of the Hope–Crosby partnership. When they could, they escaped to the nearest golf course together. Golf was fast proving an addiction to them both. Now, in recent years, Hope has been careful to say that golf is too serious a game to be interrupted by talk – at least the kind of talk that owes nothing to the speed of the ball, the condition of the greens or the quality of their swings. But it wasn't always so. It was while taking one of those breaks from shooting, Mel Shavelson recalled for me, that they played with a businessman who gave them more than just a useful tip.

'This was an old man, 'Mel Shavelson remembered, 'whom they felt sorry for and they suggested they join him for a round. Afterwards, the man took them aside and said, "Bob and Bing, you've been very nice to me, but how much do you fellers get for a movie – and how much do you have to give to the government? You're crazy working for Uncle Sam and not keeping anything for yourselves."

'They got a little suspicious when he asked them to put two thousand dollars in one of his oil wells. Somehow, though, they agreed to do so. A few months later, Bob called me into his office and showed me the cheque they had received for their share of the man's oil field – a cheque for six million dollars.'

The man was the founder of the Gilmore Petroleum Company.

Both Bing and Bob had clever business brains and, perhaps even more importantly, they both had a clever business adviser. But it is clear that Hope was the one with the sharper acumen. He was advised to put his spare cash into land

BING
CROSBY

BOB
HOPE

DOROTHY
LAMOUR

A PARAMOUNT PICTURE

ROAD TO ZANZIBAR

...UNA MERKEL · ERIC BLORE

Quite a team – even if Dorothy Lamour was always the junior partner.

and, since he had quite a lot of spare cash, there was a deal of land to buy. He took the advice and started buying up parcels of property no one else had ever thought worthwhile. It was not just a sound investment, but the start of one of the most successful property businesses the West Coast had ever known. As far as money was concerned – and he was scooping it up from his entertainment work as though it had just been invented – he could have become a multimillionaire without ever looking at another camera or talking in front of another microphone.

But the audience proved to be an equally strong addiction. As with most people, Hope liked others to like him. But more than that, he craved it. The sound of a crowd clapping or laughing at the jokes that had been prepared for his expert delivery was food and drink to him.

The remarkable thing about that is that Hope off-stage is not usually a funny man. As Arthur Marx told me, 'He's just a straight conversationalist. He can be flip, but not really funny. He would never say things George S. Kaufman would say.'

But you wouldn't know it seeing Bob perform. Probably no one since the days when Al Jolson had enjoyed the public consummation of his affair with the mob sitting out front at Broadway's Winter Garden Theater had an entertainer both needed and received such adoration. Jolson in blackface down on one knee, singing to his Mammy. Hope standing behind a microphone with script in hand.

The Pepsodent Show was incredibly successful, with Bob joking, singing and laughing, almost always with another performer of equal status sharing some of the mike time with him – if they weren't top stars, the rule was they would never get on his show – along with the regulars who were there to be his foils, fill out the bill and provide the audience with the sort of characters they sat and waited for. The most popular of these was a young man who they heard – and they had to take Bob's word for this – had a huge moustache. The fact that he also played the trombone and had a speaking/shouting voice that sounded as if the instrument was still grafted on to his lips was something they could hear for themselves. His name was Jerry Colonna.

Colonna had a small part in *Road to Singapore* and his radio audiences could then see his moustache for themselves. When they heard his voice, they knew they hadn't been cheated. Such was the power of radio in 1940.

It took just a year for a second *Road* film to be made. *The Road to Zanzibar* followed with the predictability of a Cook's tour. It was of the same pattern, but a lot better, particularly the last scene when the two are drifting on a raft. Bob chokes out in his desperation, 'I'm going to die, I'm going to die', but then Bing points to where they are drifting – New York Harbor. Bob is not pleased. 'I was about to get an Academy Award!' As we shall see, that was not just a joke.

Once more, Bob was the coward and Bing got the girl, who again was Dorothy Lamour. No longer were Bing and Bob a couple of playboys as they had been in the earlier film. Now they made no pretence of the fact that they and Lamour were on safari in deepest Africa. If there had been a script of any kind in the first place, it was obvious they were going to tear the whole thing up as they went along. They didn't just play pat-a-cake and make asides to the audience: they inserted all the jokes that they wanted precisely where they wanted them. The script was by Frank Butler and Don Hartman, but it was cheerfully augmented by whatever ad-libs they could think of – or rather what their writers could think of. Mel Shavelson was frequently asked for the odd line that could be worked into the screenplay. It didn't matter that it had practically no relevance to the action that had originally been laid down.

But Hope didn't throw his fellow actors the way that Danny Kaye did, says Shavelson. 'Bob would never do that. He would not depart from the script unless he mentioned it ahead of time.' And it need hardly be said that, when he did mention something like that, no one was going to argue the point with him.

Don Hartman himself was always modest about what he had achieved. He said once, 'You take a piece of used chewing gum and flip it at a map. Wherever it sticks, you can lay a *Road* picture. If they're nasty and menacing, it'll be a good *Road* picture. The key to the thing is menace offsetting the humour.'

There was nothing menacing about Hope, but that was not the situation with the world outside the Paramount studios.

By the time the first *Road* picture was in the theatres, Bob Hope was planning to take his first look in years at the country of his birth – go to Hitchin where his grandfather, in his nineties, was still alive and kicking anyone who thought he should be taking life easy, and to visit his birthplace, Eltham. He booked a passage on the *Queen Mary*, the only way to cross the Atlantic in 1939. The ship was crowded, so crowded that Bob was to sing – in a specially crafted new lyric to 'Thanks For The Memory' – that he was privileged to find a very nice room for himself, so nice that it had the word 'Gentlemen' on the door.

News broke while they were afloat that Neville Chamberlain had declared war on Germany. Bob was ready to cancel his planned ship's concert that Sunday night. Harry Warner, eldest of the Warner Brothers, was on board, too – and persuaded him to go ahead anyway. Rarely were Bob Hope jokes more needed.

It would not be the only trip he took on the *Queen* during the next few years. Bob liked to tell of the instructions that he said – and he swore it was true – were given by Hitler at the time: to sink the *Queen Mary* and receive a $200,000 reward. If Bob Hope was on board, the reward would go up to $300,000. There was no enemy action on that first trip – apart from any heckling that might have come from the people who didn't like the gags.

Being back in England did not convince Bob Hope that he was at heart an Englishman. He had grown up in America – America had given him his fame, his fortune and his women.

He went back to the States, the country that was very much home, ready to carry on as before in the land that was still at peace. In 1940 alone, it was estimated that Hope's income from his movies and his radio show (and the shows of other people on which he now appeared as guest star) was half a million dollars. Take the value of those dollars ahead by more than half a century and the figure moves into the stratosphere – particularly when you realize that it didn't include any of his business dealings.

It wasn't just a matter of work and the money it brought him that occupied his attention at that time. Dolores had finally come to the conclusion that she would never be pregnant and decided that the time had come to adopt a baby. They adopted a girl whom they named Linda, and the following year, they adopted a boy, Tony.

By now, Bob himself had been firmly adopted by America's top columnists. Wherever he went, he was fêted by the women in the big hats and the men who dripped cigarette ash on to their typewriters. Damon Runyon, the most caustic of writers who spent only part of his time writing about the guys and dolls of Broadway, had been on Hope's friends list ever since he had written – about 'Thanks for the Memory' – 'What a delivery, what a song, what an audience reception!' He was followed by virtually every other journalist who took Hope as the perfect demonstration of what a good, clean entertainer should be.

They liked him, so they wrote nice things about him and the public wanted to see more of a man who was quickly becoming an idol. To help publicize his movies, he went back to the world of vaudeville, gagging at cinemas in between

Bob and Dolores in England with Uncle Charles, Aunt Lucy and family, 1947.

the programmes. During one stretch in Chicago, he was doing seven shows a day and chalked up earnings of $20,000 in one week. So as not to interrupt the never-ending spiral of financial success, he arranged with NBC for the radio programme to be broadcast from whatever city he was playing that week.

The idea of taking the programme out on to the road was infectious – and so was doing live performances to his adoring public – provided he could have his script with him when he needed it. It was in March 1941 that the most infectious idea of all was put to him. 🆖

Chapter five – A GLOBAL AFFAIR

The idea was to be infectious not just to Bob Hope, but to a whole generation of top-flight entertainers – to play to the troops, young men bored out of their minds at a time, eight months before Pearl Harbor, when they thought they had nothing serious to do.

It had been done during World War One and then in a whole series of war-bond rallies, but the idea of a comedian of Bob Hope's status finding time from all his money-spinning work schedule to tell jokes – unpaid – to a load of servicemen in peace time . . . that was unheard of.

Why Hope accepted this suggestion so readily is a mystery. Even *he* had to think about it. It was totally out of character for this man who would apparently do anything for a buck and little without one. There weren't even any young women around – yet. So the conclusion has to be that he acted purely altruistically for the sake of helping the young men relieve their boredom. Either that or it was simply the magnetism of a whole new audience so hungry for entertainment that they would be the most appreciative bunch of 'customers' he had ever known.

All of the above was true. But there was a reluctance when the idea was first put to him to take his show to the March Field Army Air Corps base, not far from Los Angeles. 'He didn't want to go,' Melville Shavelson told me. 'He didn't want to take the show out of the studio because it would cost him money. Finally, he agreed only because his producer had a brother at March Field and he had promised he would bring the show up there.'

But, from the moment he got in front of the microphone at March Field, he was hooked. Pepsodent, who, it later emerged, had encouraged him to take advantage of the publicity potential the trip presented, were delighted. So were Paramount. Bob's most recent film, *Caught In The Draft*, was about army life, so the trip was useful for them, too. Did Hope allow such thoughts to come into his mind before he went? It would be churlish to say so, but none of it did do him any harm at all.

It also helped to change his life – from the moment he said, 'Good evening, ladies and gentlemen, this is Bob March Field Hope telling all the aviators, while we can't advise you on how to protect your chutes, there's nothing like Pepsodent to protect your tooths.'

By now the penny, or the cent, should have dropped. The show was being broadcast. A new pattern had been set – not just for his broadcasting but for his special kind of showmanship. He took to the service audience like a cat being offered a giant-sized bowl of cream. When the bowl was finished he licked his lips

Bob looked good in uniform. However, he was usually looking elsewhere.

The Hope 'Gypsies'. With Frances Langford, Tony Delano and Jerry Colonna.

and begged for more. When war came for America in December 1941, he was ready for all that could be thrown at him. At the same time, the army chaplains and others who were responsible for service morale let it be known that they regarded him as America's principal secret weapon at a time when things weren't going at all well.

There was talk of Hope himself being drafted into the service. The idea was vetoed immediately – and not by him. It was generally agreed that what he was doing was much more useful than driving a desk in some army base.

It was a distinction, however, that was not always appreciated. At one show, a soldier called out, 'Hi, ya slacker!'

Bob came back with a riposte that could not have been prepared by any of his writers: 'It's amazing,' he said, 'how you meet Crosby's relatives everywhere.' The heckling stung – until the house dissolved the way he hoped it would. Anyway, he always protested he would have liked to be one of the boys at the other side of the stage. 'I tried to enlist,' he protested. 'As a hostage.' Years before the irony of that statement could be apparent, it was a pretty funny line.

The routine for the shows was always the same. Bob in a semi-military uniform – with the words 'camp shows' emblazoned under an eagle on his cap badge – introduced himself by squeezing the name of the camp in between his own two names and then welcomed the others who were with him – Jerry Colonna and his moustache, the comedienne Vera Vague (her real name was Barbara Allen), a popular guitar player called Tommy Romano and Skinnay Ennis's band. Then the exciting moment, the arrival of his attractive new girl vocalist, Frances Langford. She looked at him and mocked: 'Dorothy Lamour, what has she got on me?' 'She hasn't got anything on herself,' Bob came back.

Langford was to go round the world with Bob and Colonna, doing her own share of clowning, along with singing whatever was top of the pops at the time. Together they went into the steaming jungles of the South Pacific and into the bitter cold wastes of Alaska. They performed while bombs and shells whistled around them in Africa, making do with the most rudimentary sanitary arrangements. (The army engineers were particularly delighted with a ladies' toilet they built specially for Frances, and she was, too – until she looked up at the sky and saw a pack of soldiers in the trees above. But they were there, of course, to spy on the enemy.)

It was the total bravery of the company that struck everyone. The world's worst movie coward was brave beyond imagination, joking about bullets that could so easily have ended more than his career. His team of writers had never been so busy.

Frances Langford recalled for me, 'There was the particular buzz about being there at this time, the magic of it, just being with the troops – that was the main thing. The more you did, the more you wanted to do.' And she added, 'I think we got more out of it than they did. Every show seemed to be better than the last.'

They just got into a jeep, drove through the sand of the Western Desert in North Africa 'and we'd wind up in Tunis'. She said, 'We were a family. We really felt like it. We had such a family, they called me Mother!'

The real problem for the entertainers was that they were able to go home when the shows were all over, while the boys had to stay – some of them to get killed. 'It was terrible,' she says softly.

Even today, elderly gentlemen still approach her and say that they heard her during the war. 'To them and to us all, Bob was wonderful.'

One night outside Tunis, Bob heard that there was a field hospital – a large tent – nearby. He insisted on going there. Field Marshal Rommel had other ideas. On the way, German planes flew over and strafed their convoy. Bob and Frances jumped into a nearby ditch until the planes had passed over.

'We were all scared. The sergeant who was with us said that the culvert where we were standing was used by sheep, which go there during the day to shelter from the hot sun. Bob said, "Thank God it's *sheep* that we can smell".'

She said that she has always thought he was funnier off stage than he was on.

At every wartime show, there were always surprise guests. In London and in dozens of places elsewhere, he played around with Crosby, one moment doing the *Road* show pat-a-cake routines, teasing each other and the next singing. The songs were either more of the current hits or the latest nonsense songs like 'Mairzy Dotes' – which could have been sung as 'Mares eat oats' but never was. And there was always the glamour. Bob rightly worked out that there was no better way of easing the load for the men in uniform than letting them see a few pretty girls, who were even less available than regular portions of good food.

In the heat, Frances Langford wore nothing more than a pair of thin shorts and a bra. The sight sent the sex-starved soldiers into convulsions. There were always other women on the bill, too – a speciality dancer, some guest singers. Occasionally, there would be a top star along, like Lana Turner. It was noticed, however, that the girls who got the best attention from Hope were the unknowns, girls who volunteered for the shows because they thought it would help their careers, a notion of which Bob was never one to disabuse them. He usually had other ideas of his own.

Bob Slatzer told me that, whenever Bob flew into a city, his first question was, 'Are the girls here?' When he left that city the girls stayed behind. 'There would always be new girls waiting for him' – provided either by his brother George or by other members of his party.

George had become Bob's gofer, almost his pimp. In fact, all Bob's brothers had been on his payroll from time to time. He set up the oldest, Ivor, in an hotel business. Jack became his personal manager at one time. Brother Fred had a butchery, largely financed by Bob. Jim Hope ran Bob's real-estate holdings. Sid was in farming.

Slatzer saw at first hand the way Bob looked after his brothers. 'There was a cheque for all of them every month, but I remember hearing Bob say at a funeral that he wished he had done more for them.'

But then he was always busy and never more so than when he was with the troops. He entertained at one camp where the girls weren't the main interest – an outpost of the Women's Army Corps. He got such a rousing reception that he turned around to make sure that his fly was done up. He told them he had been well looked after by their officers. 'They took me on a tour of the camp but there was one restricted area – it was where you girls hang out your underwear.'

The general feeling was that Hope loved these diversions – because they gave him better opportunities than anything else he did to indulge in what was quaintly known in those days as 'fraternization'. What was more, he could do it quite legally and without Dolores suspecting a thing.

It would be unfair, however, to think that this was his only motive. He was conscious that he was doing an enormous amount of good and not just for his own libido. When the men saw that he was willing to go into the front line, exposing himself to activity that was potentially even more fatal than a bad gag, they showed a particular respect not often accorded to civilians. Frank Sinatra was constantly made a press target in those days for precisely *not* doing what Bob Hope had taken as his duty.

He was, however, also providing great material for *The Pepsodent Show*. Time after time, the shows were broadcast, always with Bob telling jokes about the Germans or about General Patton and leaving the guys to fall down laughing over their rifles. He made very clear his own philosophy on that sort of thing. 'I am only sad when I miss a laugh. I cry right in public.'

That particular general wasn't exactly laughing himself. He had just visited an army hospital and slapped the face of a shell-shocked soldier who he thought was malingering. Overnight, the general who wore the shiny helmet and carried pearl-handled pistols had been converted by the press from everyone's hero into a dangerous disaster.

When Hope met him, Patton said plaintively, 'I want to ask you a favour. You can do me lots of good when you go back home. Tell all the people who listen to you on the radio that I'm crazy about my men, that I think they're great, that I'm very proud of them.'

There is no record of whether Bob did or did not pass on the vainglorious general's message. It wouldn't have made him particularly popular had he done so. Hope, who liked to tell the story, never filled in the end of the tale.

What really got the men delirious were jokes that mentioned the names of 'local' characters. Performing in Britain, he had to joke about the Prime Minister. He wasn't merely being topical – talking about Churchill was enough to get the audience on his side.

'I've just come back from the States,' he said once. 'You know the States? That's where Churchill lives.' Everyone knew that the Prime Minister was crossing the Atlantic more often than some people went to their corner shop – meeting Roosevelt, addressing both Houses of Congress – and it was the perfect theme for a joke. 'He doesn't exactly live there,' he corrected himself. 'He just goes to deliver Mrs Roosevelt's laundry.'

When he entertained British soldiers, he never overdid the 'I-was-born-in-England' bit – to do so, would have been to underplay his loyalty to America and his status as the man most Britons thought of as epitomizing the Yankee entertainer. But he was popular in the British Isles. For a time – particularly when American troops were filling the villages and hamlets of England preparing for D-Day – the BBC broadcast most of his *Pepsodent Show*, taking out all the commercials and any of the references the powers at Broadcasting House might have thought were the least bit suggestive. It was the total reverse of today's situation where broadcasters are given more freedom in Britain than in the USA.

Certainly, he was better known in Britain than Jack Benny, Fred Allen or Red

Skelton. Always, the reason was obvious. He was topical and he knew which jokes went with which audience. Sometimes, the jokes and the names were more basic than talk of statesmen and generals. They were the ones that would have been guaranteed to drive any available laughometer – if such things had existed at the time – off the scale. Just using the name of, say, the base cook would have the place rocking, particularly if he could mention some particular sin everyone knew about, like frying the food till it was inedible. Tell a slightly off-colour joke about the named commanding offcer and the audience was eating out of his hand.

The material got more and more off-colour the further the party got from the nearest radio transmitter. Plainly, that was how the men wanted it. But if the dirty joke really could be about one of their own, then the combination was perfect.

His secretaries – another important arm in the Hope business – were instructed to get the names for him. If there were in-jokes about any of them, Bob had to be informed. It's a secret that British pantomime performers had known for a hundred years: mention the name of a local personality or the kind of district that everyone in the audience would know about and the laughter would shake the very light bulbs in the theatre. In the theatre of war, the jokes were more appreciated than anywhere else on earth – especially when the 'boys' in the audience gave him and the other members of the party the names of loved ones to ring up after the tour was over. All the people were contacted, some of them by Bob himself.

All of them knew how much the Hope jokes had helped to ease the tension. When he introduced one of the beautiful women in his show, there was always an appropriate line, such as, 'I just want you boys to see what you're fighting for.' On another occasion he brought on the whole bevy. 'I know you'll remember girls,' he said, chewing gum, as, one by one, they stepped up to the mike and gave out their own verses to 'Thanks For The Memory'.

Usually there was at least one girl who he would later say was very sexy. 'So we had a lot in common,' he told Mel Shavelson for the *Don't Shoot* book. 'She was so nervous standing next to a sex symbol like me at the microphone, I dropped my script three times.'

Writers like Shavelson were busy reading the newspapers and the communiqués and supplying the jokes that Bob himself wove into his material, accepting some, rejecting others. They would get calls in the middle of the night or as they ate their breakfast, entertained friends to dinner or were making love to their wives or girlfriends. Hope didn't want to know. If he needed a joke on a certain subject that came to his mind, he expected to get it and there was no gainsaying that.

He was just as keen on getting the right terminology. In one show at the Long Beach naval base, Barbara Allen, still playing Vera Vague, decided the time had come to threaten one of the boys who was getting very excited when she pushed

They never relaxed, even in the air the wounded were entertained. In the South Pacific, 1944.

out her chest. 'If you get fresh with me,' she said, 'I'm going to the head of the Navy.' The audience collapsed. No one had told Allen that 'head' in naval-speak meant toilet. As a result of that, Shavelson and the other writers had to learn all the argot they could that would appeal to the audiences.

As one of Hope's later writers and movie directors, Hal Kanter, told me, 'Bob was a great editor.' In fact, that was an essential part of his skills. The material was not his own, but there was still not a chance that any of those writers could be as good as he was, no matter how long they had worked for him.

Kanter said, 'Bob can be very demanding – but in a very nice way. He has a very gentle touch making his demands. When Bob edits a script, it is taking out jokes or taking out words of a joke. Very seldom do I recall him ever rewriting a joke or suggesting a different joke. He has either a completely original thought of his own or he would take what material is given to him but perhaps say, "Cut the first two sentences".'

As a performer, he was never better than in the direst of circumstances. Frances Langford told me about the hospital trips they made, when the burnt and mangled bodies were hard to witness. Even harder to take was sometimes knowing more than the men did themselves about their condition – like discovering that one of the patients who asked her to take his hand had no arms. It happened more than once. She sang, 'Embrace me, you sweet embraceable you', and then discovered that this boy didn't have any hands. 'I had to run out into the hall and cry,' she said.

But still she sang and still Bob joked. 'Did you see my last show – or were you sick before?' he asked one patient. The team saw men before they were taken into makeshift operating theatres, and waited with them to come round after their anaesthetics.

Hope would walk into a ward full of maimed and limbless soldiers who could barely raise a smile. 'Don't all get up,' he'd say. 'Who's got the dice?' He and Jerry Colonna would jump on the beds (of patients they knew could take it) and race round the wards chasing the nurses, which was less of an ordeal than he might have made out. Seeing the broken bodies of kids who weren't yet old enough to vote was very real indeed. 'We were in a hospital in Algiers and the heat and the stench was terrible,' Bob recalled. 'I'd go from table to table watching these men going into surgery. The dedication of those doctors was amazing.'

One of the Marines he met was swathed in bandages. Through the hole that served to ring his mouth, he muttered one word, 'Maravovo'. It was the name of the Pacific island where a month or so earlier he had played for fifteen thousand Marines at one sitting. Of those, six thousand never got home.

Coping with the effects of the war he was plainly helping to win in his own way took an extraordinary effort, but he never shirked it. He said years later, 'If I hadn't gone I'd never have been able to look at myself in the mirror.'

General Eisenhower was among the first of the top brass to appreciate what Bob was doing and insisted on his own personal command performance in Algiers. He promised Bob that, after the activity of the past few nights, he could practically guarantee a peaceful rest in the days that followed. That very night, the group were awakened by bombs dropping on the harbour nearby. 'The next day,' Bob was to recall, 'I sent Ike a wire and thanked him for the rest. I said, "I'm glad I wasn't here on one of the nights when you had some action".'

Frances Langford remembered that night. 'Bob said, "Wouldn't you like to see Eisenhower's face now?" ' They sheltered in a cellar. 'And we all had a wonderful time. All the bombs were falling and the people just thought he was so great to be there.'

It wasn't the only time he was in danger. The plane carrying the Hope travelling circus made a crash landing and Bob ended up in a ditch with a fractured leg. He was taken to the field hospital, where a young Medical Corps man started working on his leg. Even a comedian could see that the man had no idea what he was doing. 'How did you get into the Medical Corps?' Bob asked him. 'You see,' said the man, 'when I first joined the army, they asked the name of my last employer. I said Dr Pepper' (the name of a popular soft drink).

In between the shows, Bob still did his radio programmes – audiences liked the army shows best of all and wrote to state their impatience if it was obvious he was broadcasting that week from the NBC studios at the corner of Sunset and Vine. He had also still been making his movies while the world was at war, both before and during the American involvement. The two films with Paulette Goddard had been imensely successful and Paramount wanted a third. This turned out to be *Nothin' But The Truth*. Hope and Goddard looked good together and there were no stories about their romancing each other off the screen. Even for the 1940s, this movie had a tired old story – a stockbroker bets a fortune that he can avoid telling even the most innocent little lie for twenty-four hours – but the public seemed to like it. They might have liked it again fifty-seven years later when Jim Carrey remade the story, but that remake proved something that nobody intended – just how subtle Hope's own performance had been.

His new status had a lot to do with the love and affection in which the American people now held him. He came home from one of his overseas trips saying how unused he was to being Mount Rushmore. After nearly every trip, he gave a press conference. One newsreel showed an exhausted-looking, unshaven Hope, telling the reporters that he had been more moved by his experiences than he could possibly say. There were no jokes.

Hope was one of Paramount's most important stars – even if in box office appeal, and to his obvious chagrin, he didn't quite meet the sort of success that Bing Crosby had – and he was earning what was for the times good money, round about $20,000 a picture. It wasn't enough. Both he and Louis Schurr reckoned he ought to get $50,000.

That he got more cash at this time was due to Sam Goldwyn, who had the bright idea of making a film starring Bob. Goldwyn was not the kind of man to be put off by mere details like studio contracts – as long as those contracts were not with him. This was before Danny Kaye had joined his 'stable', and he hadn't had a top comedy star since Eddie Cantor had had people queuing to see his films. He was sure that Bob Hope represented the precise formula he wanted.

He had just borrowed Gary Cooper for his new film, *The Westerner,* and could see no reason why he couldn't do a deal for Hope, too. Neither could Paramount – to most people's amazement. Bob himself said he had no objection, provided the moguls didn't try to sew him up in the usual studio-star deal: the 'borrower' pays an enormous sum for the services of the star who, in turn, gets no more than his usual salary.

Bob bided his time and with his usual business acumen found just the right moment to discuss details with the man who firmly believed that an oral contract was never worth the paper it was written on. He probably also thought that Hope,

BOB HOPE

The weather was just another enemy to be faced.

like most comedians, didn't really know much about figures – the kind on a balance sheet, that is – and was as malleable as the rest. Bob could have told him that they had all passed a lot of water since those days.

The right moment for the business discussion that Bob knew he needed came in the midst of the tour that Paramount had organized to publicize *The Westerner* in Texas. Bob was making personal appearances all over the state as MC. On one of them, as he knew, the guest appearance would be by Sam Goldwyn himself. Cleverly, he had engineered a line in the mogul's script in which he told him, in front of the two or three thousand people in the audience at Fort Worth, how much he wanted to have Hope in a Goldwyn film. 'How about it Bob?' he asked.

It was a question that he couldn't avoid answering, a gift from the Hollywood heaven. 'OK, Sam,' he said, 'let's talk money.'

'Not now,' said Goldwyn totally thrown by what he would have recognized as the chutzpah of the comedian, who clearly was not being funny at that moment. 'Yes, right now,' he said. 'Let's just lie down here on the stage and talk deals until we arrive at something. I want a hundred grand.'

I wanna tell ya…

Sam wasn't happy, not happy at all. He didn't like negotiating with a mere actor and he certainly didn't at all like negotiating in public. He was thrown. 'I only pay Gary Cooper—' Imagine that, Sam Goldwyn about to reveal how much he paid a top star – on the day that that top star's latest movie was being premièred.

Hope was enjoying the fact that he looked as if he was about to win and was prepared to be rude. 'Who cares what you pay that drugstore cowboy,' he asked. Had Cooper been there at that moment – and the wonder was that he wasn't – he would have been mortified. Goldwyn was pretty upset himself. Particularly when he realized he had to fork out $75,000 for the privilege, the sum on which they finally settled. But that said a great deal about Bob Hope's business brain and the value he put upon himself. He might have a top agent and the best financial advisers his money could provide, but, when it came to a face-to-face deal, braving Bob Hope was like facing a lion in his own den. It was a big man's game and Hope was its master. *bh*

Chapter Six – THEY GOT ME COVERED

'**F**ish don't applaud,' Bob Hope said when asked why he once rushed home from a fishing expedition that had been intended as a rest cure. For him, taking a rest was equivalent to putting up a sign that said he was going out of business. That wouldn't have been possible. With all the deals running around his head, it was as though he regarded himself as one of the American states – that is, one of the important ones. If he packed up, the Union would fall apart. As if to back up that thought, he started buying up property in the San Fernando Valley as though he were in the midst of some kind of gold rush, which in a way he was. He had bought himself a house in Toluca Lake, one of the plushiest parts of the Los Angeles area. It was a magnificent house, spreading out seemingly for miles, but Hope immediately began extending it, suite after suite of living rooms, a dining room that Phyllis Diller, the oddball comedienne, insists can seat 500 people, dens, guest accommodation and the kind of office space that befitted a man who always seemed as if he were ready to take on the President of General Motors. To this day, it remains Hope's favourite home. With a three-hole golf course in the grounds, it could hardly be anything else.

'He owned more land in the valley than the United States government,' said Mel Shavelson – and he wasn't joking. Bob took his bank manager on a car ride through what was one of the district's prime real-estate locations – pointing out which land he himself already owned and what he was going to buy. He bought the lot, mile after mile of it. To do otherwise, he seemed to say, would have been a kind of treason.

It started out as a means of helping one of his brothers. As we have seen, he had been helping the family since he first became dazzlingly successful – not keeping them in gold, necessarily but, to paraphrase one of his friends, in a degree of brass-and-gold plate.

Jim Hope didn't seem to have an enormous amount of talent, so Bob gave him a business selling real-estate. Except that he couldn't sell anything. The only solution was to put the elder brother in charge of his own interests. Officially, that is. Bob Hope knew every penny that he was spending and every nickel he was making, but someone had to keep the books.

Having a lookout for his business affairs took the same kind of eye he put to his scripts – the ones he read when he was in a radio studio or playing to the troops, to work out precisely what was right for him and what he could not possibly do.

He could spot a good deal the way he could identify a good joke – or a good girl.

Bob and Bing and their shared passion (when there were no girls around, that is). In England, 1952.

The notion of Hope and girls went together as obviously and as regularly as Hope and golf – or Hope and Crosby.

There's a great deal of evidence to show that the two men were not just rivals for the hand of Dorothy Lamour – or the rest of her. They were constantly trying to outsmart each other off screen, too.

'I think they were friendly for a time,' Bob Slatzer told me. 'But I never thought they really liked each other. There was an intense rivalry between them. What Bing had, Bob wanted.'

They even had a rivalry over drink – but not for long. Crosby was a well-known drinker; Hope drank much less, but for a very brief period he had a drink problem of his own, although he dried himself out before any serious damage could be done. (It has been suggested that he loved the flavour of the limes growing on his estate, so he began to enjoy them a little too much – mixing them with gin.)

On most things, they were like small boys fighting over a toy. Years later, when Bing won an Oscar, Bob wanted one, too – more than anything else in the world. He was master of ceremonies at countless Academy Award presentations but the little statuette for a movie part always eluded him. 'We call Oscar nights Passover in our home,' he joked, although, when Crosby won his for *Going My Way*, he was not at all amused.

Bob had had awards from the Academy of Motion Picture Arts and Sciences, a gold medal in 1940, a life membership and a silver plaque, but not yet a statuette. Always the bridesmaid, never the bride. He continued to joke about it for as long as he was able to tell jokes. And there was usually a ready explanation . 'After all,' he once said, 'you can make great pictures. You think you have made a very good film and it competes with *Gone With The Wind* or *Boom Town*. So you don't win – and feel about as important as the dialogue director on *Deep Throat*.'

That might or might not have been a line he wrote for himself. He said it spontaneously on the Michael Parkinson BBC chat show – but then that was just part of his art, dragging just the right joke out of the mental computer at just the right moment.

Mel Shavelson is convinced that Bob is a naturally funny man. He has just never had time to write everything for himself. And there were the serious moments for him, which talking about that terrible business of the Oscars always was. Not that he was unprepared, should the miracle have ever happened. He would admit he still had his acceptance speech ready. 'I have had it for so long, it's in Latin.'

Crosby didn't have to wait long at all for his awards. In truth, Hope wouldn't have minded his friend having any toy, provided he had the same thing to play with in the nursery. For them that nursery was the Paramount lot or wherever else they played. They wanted to score off each other on the golf course, too. When there was a Bing Crosby tournament, there had also to be a Bob Hope one. When they were not competing in serious tournaments, they would face each other on the links of the Lakeside Club, one of the most popular in Hollywood (a club that was restricted to white Gentiles, a fact that does not appear to have worried either of them).

Crosby's main investments were connected with horses. He had a hefty share in the Del Mar race track on the Californian coast – 'Where the surf meets the turf' – and owned race horses, all of which befitted his image as the colour-blind man who wore odd socks and ghastly check shirts, and was never seen without a race card in his hands. Bob, on the other hand, looked at his real-estate interests for money and his golf for fun – the kind of serious fun that meant anyone not taking the game as seriously as he did might just as well have stolen a joke.

Crosby, he would admit, was always a better golfer than he was. The champion Lee Trevino once pointed out that Bob needed four putts to get the ball in a hole. 'Well,' he said, 'I like putting.'

To watch a game in which Hope played was to see a Hope show. He didn't always see it like that, but the people who thronged what the golfers like to call the 'gallery' did. 'I think I play the game seriously, but I get too many laughs. I play a strange shot and people laugh.' Which no comedian ought to dismiss lightly.

Sometimes, the gallery offers sympathy. Once, a crowd watched Bob knock a ball straight into the woods beyond the course. 'I was just tapping my club when an old lady looked at me and said, "Don't you worry honey. It's not your regular business".'

He tried his hand at horses, too, but the magic of the turf eluded him. *Time* magazine reported that he went with Bing to the track one day, bet a fair amount, and won – but when he started losing packed up and went home. Crosby decided this was an opportunity to show just how real his friendship with Bob really was. He was going to nip in the bud any suggestion that Hope was a four-letter word meaning mean. He instantly penned a letter to the magazine, which might or might not have been written by a press agent spying an opportunity to plug both men.

'My friend Bob Hope is anything but cheap. He does an average of two benefits a week. His price for a personal appearance would be about $10.000, so he gives away $20,000 every week of his life. Is that cheap?'

The magazine wasn't willing to leave things at this. '*Time* agrees with Bing,' said an editorial footnote. 'However, Bob Hope, from time to time, has been known to put undue pressure on a nickel.'

Mel Shavelson could have agreed with that. When Sam Goldwyn took him on to his staff, a Bob Hope film was his first assignment. 'That means I won't have to pay him the ten thousand dollars he gets for his writers,' said the mogul contentedly. Mel was less satisfied. 'Bob always told us he got *five* thousand dollars – which shows how you become a billionaire.'

Shavelson told me of the time writers started betting Bob $5 that one of their gags would work. 'So Bob deliberately loused it up – and took their five dollars.'

With Syd Field in London (1947).

He often talked about money, but as only rich people do. In one movie, he looked quizzically at the audience. 'We haven't got any money,' he said plaintively – then added, 'That's for Washington.'

There would be a few problems with authorities in years to come, but nobody could accuse Bob of not paying his taxes at this time. It wouldn't have fitted at all well into the character of the man who was doing so much to help national wartime morale – and that of his own bank balance, which wasn't exactly damaged by anything he did on screen.

He and Crosby don't seem to have ever got into any financial rows, no matter how many business deals they had together. One was as cute as the other when it came to business deals. And when it came to women they played the same game with the same stakes – and always won. They discussed 'form' over lunch in the studio dining room and gave each other tips, as though they were talking about one of Bing's race horses. In a way that's how both regarded women – as fillies who either took to the going or didn't.

Arthur Marx told me of the time that Bing went into hospital to have his appendix removed. He was treated by a beautiful young nurse who was not just rounded in all the right places but provided certain personal services that are not normally covered by health-insurance policies. When he came out of the hospital, he suggested that Bob might like to be treated by her, too – so he checked into the same hospital and asked to be attended by the same nurse. 'Hope wasn't sick or anything at the time, but he checked into the hospital the next day and spent three days there with the same nurse'.

He seems to have been cured of whatever it was that he claimed ailed him, too.

It was no more than happened in the studio and on the battle front – which was only occasionally a battle between Bob and the girls. He and Bing didn't even fight among themselves for a particular busty, hippy beauty. There were always enough to go around.

Usually, the girls were willing accomplices – very willing indeed. A chance to play on the Bob Hope show held out the possibilities of a showbiz career and Bob was known to frequently allow them walk-on roles in his radio show, as his part in any agreement they may have had on the way to his casting couch.

Military policemen guarded the corridors whenever Bob and Bing were in army barracks. Hope arranged the same facility for any other male star wanting what he considered to be his just deserts for helping the war effort. The only other people allowed to penetrate the barrier were the girls who were sleeping with them.

Arthur Marx told me, 'A friend of mine was a writer who worked on Bob's radio show. He would tell me stories about how Mr Hope would take a writer with him when he would do a camp show out in Azouza or one of those places. And then [the writer] would give him a couple of ad-libs for the show. But then if Bob happened to meet a girl in the show or a groupie who happened to be hanging around and he wanted to go off with her, he'd dump the writer right there and the writer would have to get back to Hollywood on his own. Usually about four o'clock in the morning. By bus.'

But there was always work for those writers. They offered something that the girls couldn't possibly provide, those girls who came to him along with the occasional Big Idea.

Marx told me Bob chose to make one film that he himself had written simply because it was the thinnest script in the pile of papers before him. He couldn't be bothered to take on anything that looked more daunting. 'He took it home and read it and liked it. That was how he decided to read it – it was the thinnest.'

He remembered how Hope would eat in front of his writers and never offer them any of the food. Or he would send for a can of beer for two men – and split the contents between the two of them.

Bob wouldn't have wanted that sort of treatment for himself. At Paramount, he demanded to be fawned over. It is quite usual for big stars to expect that their dressing rooms be completely redecorated whenever they move in. In Hope's, there was always an extra bed behind an extra door as well as a gold basket containing an ice bucket, always stocked with a new bottle of champagne. There was a reason for that. Bob had an additional feature in his dressing room that fitted in perfectly with his champagne bucket.

There was an anteroom which had to have its own door on to the back of the lot. This had to be furnished with a couch on which he could 'rest'. The people who were shown into the 'resting' room had to fulfil certain qualifications – be female, young, beautiful and willing to 'rest' with him. He also had to have a telephone in the room – so that he could be informed of any unwelcome guest. Once Dolores came unannounced. The anteroom door was locked and the girl of the afternoon ushered unceremoniously (if not undressed) into the street outside. Dolores had to make an appointment if she wanted to see Bob at the studio, claimed Jan King, later Hope's confidential secretary. He had five of those secretaries, including one whom a pressman asked Bob to give a squeeze at her farewell party . 'This isn't my squeezing secretary,' he responded.

In an interview given to the tabloid newspaper *The Globe*, Jan King was quoted as saying that she and Bob had code names for the various girls in his life.

As the war went on, the number of starlets increased. Girls like Marie (The Body) MacDonald fitted the kind of image he wanted for his shows. He liked them to be there to augment the comedy, so that the audiences would be in a good mood for his jokes. It was the reverse of the usual situation in girl shows where the comedian was barely tolerated while the men out front waited for the women to get out of something more comfortable.

There was never any doubt who was the star. But even Bob Hope had to accept that when he and Bing were together it was, of necessity, an equal partnership.

In 1942, Hope and Crosby made their third *Road* film. *The Road to Morocco* ('Like Webster's Dictionary, we're Morocco-bound') was the best of the lot. The formula was exactly as always. But there were more than a few choice moments – like the time Bing and Bob have the same dream, in superimposed bubbles over their heads, with one character moving from one bubble to the next as though they were both in the same play.

The story ... well, as in all the best Hope–Crosby movies, you worked it out for yourself in between the gags. Again Dorothy Lamour was alluring and again Bob lost her. But the real winner in this film was the talking camel – the one that Bob looks straight in the eye just as it spits into his.

It hadn't been planned – how could you plan for a camel to spit in anyone's eye? – and, when the beast decided to get his own back on those characters who had moved in on his part of the world, the camera was conveniently turning.

You always knew where the 'Road' was leading. This one to Morocco.

Everyone agreed that it had to stay. It was the best in-joke Hollywood had seen for a long time. The camel was even given lines to say at the end – with a little help from the animation department. There were those who said they were the most intelligent in the whole movie.

'I remember it as great fun,' said Anthony Quinn, who had once again been in the midst of a *Road* picture, this time playing a sheikh – the one with designs on Lamour that were not exactly the kind planned by the costume department.

His is a sheikh with a sharp Arabic tongue. When he realizes that Crosby is his rival for the sarong girl's affections, he whispers sweet nothings to him – like calling him 'the moon-faced son of a one-eyed donkey'. Hope is quick to defend his hapless colleague. 'I wouldn't let him call me that,' he advises. 'Even if there *is* a resemblance.'

He may have been thwarted in the end, but Bob still fancied himself as the great lover. 'I'm going to be a pasha, with the emphasis on the pash,' he says in a line made to measure for the Morocco locale. They traded insults the way other men swapped jokes – and Bob Hope was never going to let anyone have *his* jokes, despite the efforts of the writers to make Bing funny, too. When Bing did have a

With Madeleine Carroll, in My Favourite Blonde.

funny line, Hope would answer with a reference to something that Crosby didn't like – such as his age. 'You've got everything I've got,' he says in one line in the film, 'and you've had it much longer.'

It could be argued that it was Bob who had Dorothy Lamour for much longer. Professionally, they had gone back a long way, but it always remained a professional relationship, which may account for the way that both Bing and Bob never let her form part of a threesome when there wasn't a camera turning.

'Dotty was good in the pictures,' Anthony Quinn recalled for me, 'but neither Bing nor Bob took her very seriously off screen.' Lamour had a reputation for being something of a prude to the point of refusing to dance close-up with Quinn. They knew that she was off limits and, since there were plenty of young ladies who were not, it did not matter to either of them.

Even if Bob had no romantic designs on them, he was the one who picked his own leading ladies. For *My Favourite Blonde*, his other 1942 film, he chose Madeleine Carroll, whom he did regard as his favourite blonde. He had seen her unfastening her stockings in *The Thirty-Nine Steps*, and was totally smitten. The difference between Bob Hope and others who were captivated by her allure was that he could do something about it. He talked about her on *The Pepsodent Show*. It got to the point where he only had to say the words 'Madeleine Carroll' for the studio audience to go crazy, wolf whistling one moment and laughing till their seats shook the rest of the time.

Eventually, Carroll herself got the point. She was getting a lot of free publicity for doing precisely nothing, so asked Bob if she could appear on his show. Not only could she appear, he said – it seemed to be the answer to his prayers – but he had an idea for a movie with her. It turned out to be one of his more inspired ideas, one of those notions that continually proved the point that he was totally in charge of his career. As far as Madeleine herself was concerned, it gave her the chance of one of the best parts in Hollywood.

His intentions, he could protest with a degree of sincerity, were again in this case strictly professional. 'Madeleine Carroll was much impressed with me,' he would say. 'So much so, that she married Sterling Hayden right in the middle of the picture. However, she did marry him secretly, which cut down on the wave of mass suicides which would otherwise have followed.'

He might also have said that the secrecy helped him save face among the Hollywood set who knew of his reputation. What would it have looked like for him to have a beautiful woman falling at his feet – yes, his feet – in a movie and not taking full advantage of the situation off screen, too?

At least, Dolores must have been pleased. In public she had to demonstrate that she was proud of her husband, even if he didn't show the same sort of pride in what she had achieved. She was – in fact still is – a very pleasant singer who would not have scared away any members of the audience who were watching Bob's films, except that the girls in those movies were usually prettier. And in truth, she never minded that Bob was the one with the great success.

As for *My Favourite Blonde*, she had to be pleased with the reaction of the critics and public to a film that, to this day, has to rank as one of his best. Hope was a burlesque player, while Carroll played a woman on a train and in distress – which gave him all the chances he needed to show just how distressed he himself could be when mixed up with a bunch of polished spies, including the always evocative Gale Sondergaard. If the Nazis really wanted to choose a woman spy who actually looked the part, Gale had to be their model. She scared the pants off

Bob's character, and the audience, too – which again helped to solidify his screen image.

It was pretty clever giving him such a definite character, one that barely changed from one movie to the next. The only thing audiences wanted to be different was the jokes. The public had got to like the coward who had funny lines to say – like 'Let's get out of here before my knees beat each other to death.' They might not have admitted it, but most of them would have had their knees knocking at the same speed – without the funny lines to say. Even in wartime, there weren't many real-life heroes.

It didn't affect their relationship with the man they laughed at on the radio week after week. They knew that he was doing some pretty brave things in the war zones. Showing he was afraid when a gun was pointing at him made him all the more acceptable. He was becoming established as that most-loved comedian, which didn't do his film career any harm at all.

The script of *My Favourite Blonde* by a quartet of Hollywood's best writing talent – Don Hartman, Frank Butler, Norman Panama and Melvin Frank – interspersed jokes into the story line so naturally that people could accept Bob as simply a funny man who got into dangerous scrapes.

It was to be the first of another one of those series that marked the Hope career – and again showed how wise he had been in not restricting his film work to a particular partnership. As Fred Astaire once told me, 'a team sounds like a pair of horses'. But, successful or not, Bob Hope wasn't going to tie himself to a single collection of movies any more than he was about to limit his appearances to playing solely with Bing Crosby, no matter how well they went together.

It didn't mean that he and Bing wouldn't always joke about each other and that barely a live appearance or a radio show happened without one mentioning the other's name.

When I interviewed Hope in the 1960s in his Savoy Hotel suite, he sat looking out at the River Thames, of which he had a splendid view from his drawing room window. As we talked, a large barge went past. 'It's carrying Crosby's money,' he quipped. Money was as important as ever.

The two of them did one show after the other. Once, on Crosby's programme, Bob began the proceedings by saying, 'Good evening, ladies and gentlemen. All right Crosby, throw me a straight line and let's get this egg rolling.'

They did a routine, allegedly recalling how they met. Crosby had a broken-down car, Hope worked at a garage. 'I think the body's got a wiggle,' said Crosby. Bob answered, 'I know all about body wiggles. I used to sell candy in a burlesque show.' Yes, even if the world was at war, it was a more innocent, protected age.

Bing noticed his friend had green stains on the arms of his jacket. Had he been leaning too close to the pool table? No, said Bob. 'I was looking down a gopher hole, looking for your Hooper ratings.'

Hope had finally beaten Crosby to the number-one ratings slot. 'You're on top!' said Bing, generously. 'Thank you,' said Bob. 'Thank you.'

Bob had plenty of reason to give thanks – not least for his movies. *Louisiana Purchase* was a remake of the Irving Berlin stage show of the same name, which convincingly merged music with political satire.

Star-Spangled Rhythm was one of those films that wartime Hollywood loved so much – a chance to bring in practically every star on a studio's current payroll. In this case, Paramount wheeled out Bob along with Betty Hutton, Bing Crosby, Dorothy Lamour, Paulette Goddard and just about everyone they could think of, with practically no story to worry about. It was one of the better portmanteau movies of the time.

Then came *They Got Me Covered*, which Bob also used as the title for the first of a series of autobiographies. He had found out that writing books was a money-spinner, so why let anyone else write them for him? Actually, that is precisely what happened. His writers, who might have got fed up with kicking their heels while they had only a weekly radio show and whatever was the current movie to work on, were told to produce a book. That, too, would go on for years – with Bob taking all the credit, just as he did when he performed on the air. Suddenly he was as good an author as he was an actor.

On stage, or before a microphone, he continued to show perfectly that his contribution was being able to put over other people's work as only he could do. But the *written* word? Well, you sat in your favourite chair and, as you read 'his' words, you could almost hear Bob speaking them. That was just part of the Bob Hope magic – and that of his writers.

Those writers never ceased to be important and he always recognized the fact. 'I'd get a call at three o'clock in the morning,' Mel Shavelson told me. 'It was always Bob and he'd say, "This is a NAFT." A NAFT stood for "Need a few things".' Like 'I've got a personal appearance tomorrow and I must have a collection of jokes by ten o'clock.' If he said 'Goodnight', the writers were lucky. They knew their contracts seemed to say – to Bob at least – that he could call them at any time of the night or day and that when he was ready he would be prepared to choose and, of course, always to edit.

But Shavelson says, 'We learned that supplying Bob with material had nothing to do with earning a living. At least, it had something to do with earning *his* living, but not ours.'

Every time he went into a film, jokes and script had to suit his own idea of his talents. Some worked, some did not. *Let's Face It* was an attempt to bring a successful Broadway show to the screen, a show about soldiers. Bob may have seemed perfect casting, except that it wasn't the perfect vehicle. Danny Kaye had had an immense success with the stage version, but Hollywood wasn't yet prepared to take a chance with a man they considered to be an unknown. (It would be just a year before Kaye himself would hit it big with a not dissimilar story called *Up In Arms*.) But the storyline was made for Danny and he should have been allowed to make the screen transfer himself.

There was, however, one thing about Bob Hope that separated him from a swathe of American comics who now more than ever depended on other people to put words into their mouths: once he accepted a joke, he took full responsibility for it, good or bad. Dennis Goodwin, a British writer who joined his joke factory in the 1950s, told me, 'If a joke played well, he'd tell you. On the other hand, if one failed, you never heard from him about it. If he accepted a joke, it was his fault if it didn't go down and he never tried to say anything else.'

Hal Kanter told me much the same thing. 'He blamed himself for choosing a gag that fell flat. He never did blame anybody. He would reject things out of hand. He would say, "Come on, I think you can do better than that," but he never, once he had accepted it, blamed anybody for its failure.'

For *The Princess and the Pirate*, Hope had the twin advantages of Mel Shavelson officially writing alongside Don Hartman, the producer – and the fact that this was a costume movie. He loved appearing for the first time in velvet and ruffles, even if he was much of the time on the run. 'I think it was his vaudeville background,' Mel told me. 'We based his part on a quick-change artist in vaudeville who used to run behind the screens and come out in a different costume each time.'

The picture was made by Sam Goldwyn – who looked at the costume worn by Walter Slezak in one scene and said, in one of the best lines not included in the script, 'You look very periodical.'

Hope was happy with the film. Said Shavelson: 'I think he was anxious to do movies because he felt that it was much easier work than doing a weekly radio show. But he would never have got by with just making movies, because he needed that live audience.'

Bob's co-star was the then highly popular Virginia Mayo. It is reasonable to imagine that she was not so popular with Bob Hope. 'I didn't like the way he kept making references to ladies' breasts,' she told me. 'He would say, "Are you a melon – or a grapefruit?" I didn't care for that.'

Bob always took that sort of reaction in his stride. After all, he had plenty to choose from. And that went for his material, too. Even Mayo remembers laughing at jokes that he would order for his script like a housewife calling for groceries. They'd come up with the goods within the hour.

Sometimes the goods came in the shape of a girl to whom he wanted to be introduced. Dolores wasn't around to cause any problems. 'She realized it was a workshop,' Virginia remembers.

There were no complaints about one of Hope's best jokes. It was in a bar scene in his next *Road* movie, the one that took him and Bing to *Utopia*. They were a

Bob acknowledging the advantage Jack Benny had over him – he could play the fiddle.

couple of prospectors in the Yukon. They were surrounded by a gang of the toughest-looking, unshaven individuals they had ever had to face. Bing calls out to the barman for 'a couple of fingers of rot-gut'. Bob, the yellow-belly who still believed that a snarl through his teeth was all that was needed to bring him to the level of the devil, finds his own way of not being outdone. 'I'll have lemonade,' says Bob, at which point the entire saloon glares in disgust '...in a dirty glass'.

In one scene they had to be confronted by a killer bear. This was a real bear and they were in the growling line themselves, no stand-ins or stuntmen as they clambered under a rug, the way the script required. There they were, two lumps under the carpet facing a big grizzly bear that bared its teeth and went 'Grrr...' 'And,' said Bob, 'we had a laundry problem.'

When Bing finally got out from under the rug, he let suitably loose with his language. 'I've never heard such words', said Hope, 'from a man who had played a priest.'

For a time, the movies never stopped.

Bob himself would have been more likely to hold on to his dog collar. Melville Shavelson told me, 'One of the things that separate him from most of the other comics is that Bob has never in public spoken a four-letter word.'

He might have done so, had he seen what happened the day after the bear episode. The animal's trainer had his arm torn off.

The film typified the relationship between the two male stars and the omnipresent Dorothy Lamour. One morning Hope and Crosby decided they preferred the idea of a charity tournament at the Lakeside golf course to the hot lights of the studio where they and Dorothy were due to film the movie's big musical number. Lamour wasn't let in on the secret. She spent two or three hours in make-up and faced the indignity of having to be eased into a tight dress with the equivalent of a whaleboned shoehorn while they were clowning around at the charity game. She relaxed for lunch and then went back to work. They were still not there. So she got out of her dress, wiped off her make-up – egged on by Gary Cooper, who happened to be in the Paramount studio at the same time – and settled for a good book. That was when Bob and Bing rang – complaining that she wasn't at their beck and call.

If anyone *was* at Bob Hope's beck and call, it was the audience for his movies and radio shows – even if Crosby was the one who was constantly being voted America's most popular movie actor. When Bing compounded that felony by winning his Oscar for *Going My Way* Bob wasn't exactly the easiest person to approach. As he said, it was Passover that year, not a holiday for him to enjoy.

There were stories of an intense jealousy engulfing him and for a time the friendship that was so public on screen dimmed considerably. Bob couldn't take the fact that Crosby had achieved something that he had manifestly failed to do.

For the first time, too, he wasn't exactly Paramount's favourite person. He demanded a script that could possibly earn him an Academy Award. Instead, they had him down to make a comedy called *Duff's Tavern*. He didn't like the script and failed to turn up for filming. The result was that the studio subjected him to the indignity suffered by every other contract player who didn't fulfil the requirements of that contract. They put him on suspension.

He could either react by playing the naughty boy and standing in the corner or get on with his own thing. It's fair to say that Bob Hope was in a mood to play naughty – and get on with entertaining his troops. Which was precisely how he saw his favourite audience. They were *his* troops. And he was *their* star.

As always, he was sure that he would equally command the loyalty of the young women who accompanied the party. Very occasionally, they refused to comply. Dorothy Lamour and Madeleine Carroll were important enough not to suffer from the consequences. Arthur Marx tells the story of one girl on the tour who was not so fortunate. According to the writer, Hope decided to punish her for failing in what he considered to be her basic duty. He made sure that she wouldn't be in a position to refuse him again. The plane out of the remote island where the troupe were performing took off without the recalcitrant young lady. She was stranded and left to find her own way home.

Not so Frances Langford. She told me of the time she sang 'I'm In The Mood For Love' at a Hope show. A soldier stood up in the crowd and shouted, 'You've come to the right place, honey.' Bob would say it got the biggest laugh he ever heard.

Naturally, Bob didn't allow some stories to get out. He was too concerned for his public image. Much more important was for the public to know that he was doing his bit – and to this end he allowed as many war photographers and newsreel cameramen as possible to film his activities. These included embarking on a series of shows for the entertainment industry's 'Victory Caravan', which raised money for war bonds. A newspaper had dubbed it that in a headline and Bob was delighted to go along with the idea.

His only concern when war ended was whether he could keep the following he had built up among the troops once they were back in civilian life.

Chapter Seven - THE FACTS OF LIFE

The troops were the best audience in the world for Bob Hope, and the war was undoubtedly his finest hour, although he would have many more hours that were fine enough for him. But playing to men in uniform was very special. Mel Shavelson told me, 'It was said that, if there wasn't a war on somewhere, Hope would start one. But the risks he took in bringing his shows to the fighting front were real, and so was his sympathy for the wounded.'

But when you have been so big, so important, the worry has to come: how long can it last? It was, to quote a later Bob Hope film, one of the facts of life. Undoubtedly, the things he had been doing – like radio and his ever-growing list of movies – had to be stepped up. And they were. On radio, Harry Truman and everything he did had to be included in his joke file and once more he had only to mention the words 'White House' for people to expect to laugh long and loud – and they were never disappointed.

It was the beginning of Bob's role as the Presidents' Favourite Comedian. He could say things about the chief executive that few others would dare to do. He once said, 'if this were Russia, I'd be master of ceremonies in a salt mine.' And then the tongue went firmly back into his cheek: 'Nowhere else in the world does free speech pay so well.'

It paid to the point that when they were building the freeway near his home, he had enough pull with the politicians to have a slip road built close to the house.

When Eisenhower became President, he began another one of the great Hope traditions – he played golf with the man in the White House. As Bill Clinton would say, 'One of the perks of this job is that you get to play golf with Bob Hope.'

Surprisingly, Les Brown, who conducted the orchestra on Bob's radio and overseas shows, saw it from a different angle. 'I think it's good politics for a president to know Bob Hope and I think it's good business for Bob Hope to know presidents.'

Bob was Ike's partner in their first game – and they lost, largely because Hope went round in over eighty. The next day, he played against the President – and won. Eisenhower looked him squarely in the face as though he were a recalcitrant junior officer. 'Why didn't you play like that yesterday?' he asked. For once, even Bob Hope was stumped for words.

It didn't happen on stage. He was ready to joke about the game – and Ike's habit of using a 'short Democrat for a tee'. His audience knew how to react to his jokes and how Bob himself would react to them. If people weren't still practically

With Peter Lorre in My Favourite Brunette - *telling him to find a decent suit.*

drowning out the first line of a new joke because they were still laughing at the last one, something was seriously wrong.

The routine never changed, but the jokes always did. You never heard the same Bob Hope story twice – not unless there was the same news in the paper two days running, which was rather more likely than hearing Hope repeat a routine. He did, however, now begin repeating a catchphrase – not deliberately: it came suddenly and became as much a part of conversation as of his act. 'Well, I want to tell ya. . . ' he'd say, and he really didn't have to tell anything, other than the next gag. Or, 'Let me tell ya. . . ' He used it the way other people dot the phrase 'you know' through their speech. He didn't even know what he was saying half the time but before long it was expected and people loved to hear it. If he didn't say, 'Well, I want to tell ya. . . ' something was seriously bothering him.

This was a man who longed to perform and that meant performing well. 'You've got to be a ham,' he said. 'I sleep on a hook at night.'

He didn't have much bothering him in the movie stakes, it has to be said. His first two postwar films were humdingers. After *The Princess and the Pirate*, he had got the bug for costume pictures and *Monsieur Beaucaire* was as funny as anything he had done before. *The Road To Rio*, however, was worth travelling along, even if the jokes were not memorable enough to get into the Hope canon. As the critic James Agee wrote, the picture had 'enough laughs to pass the time easily and to remind you how completely, since sound came in, the American genius for movie comedy has disintegrated'. It did, however, boast the Andrews Sisters, who were never exactly beautiful, and their songs accompanying Bing tended to blunt the next Hope joke.

Dorothy Lamour was around, too, as always. And so was Hope's joke factory, or rather its former members, who were now considered to be nonresident experts, always available to be brought in to add jokes and punch to scripts written by other people, not always to the delight of those original writers.

Mel Shavelson remembered: 'He would take these jokes to the producer to be added to the screenplay and the producer would always throw them out. So Bob would just slide the pages between the pages of his script. Then when it came to the point, he was always very able to apparently ad-lib them. They always broke up the crew and, when they did, there was no way the producer could chuck them out.'

When he 'ad-libbed' to a Don Hartman script, things started to get nasty. Hartman was on the set when Bing and Bob were throwing in a whole succession of supposed ad-libs. 'Don,' Bob called out to him, ' if you recognize any of your lines, shout "Bingo".'

Hartman was not impressed – or amused. He shouted to Bob, 'Follow the script, or I'll put you back in the trunk.' Nobody had ever gone that far before. It was one thing sharing a trade – and open – secret that Bob Hope needed writers to provide

Casanova's Big Night. *The bicycle shows just how versatile he could be.*

him with material and that he was merely mouthing their words, but it was quite another to call him a ventriloquist's dummy.

The Paleface didn't provide that sort of problem. It was one of the classic Hope movies and as important to his story as practically anything he ever did. Painless Potter, the dentist who somehow manages to marry a Calamity Jane played by Jane Russell, was classic casting – especially since he was so obviously not the man to marry a gun-toting girl who had only to thrust her bosom his way for him to take cover. The flying bullets were not to be sneezed at, either. It was perhaps the best strictly comedy film he ever made and had his best song since 'Thanks For The Memory'. 'Buttons and Bows' became the really big hit of 1948. But, most importantly, the film itself showed just how clever he was, a radio and personal-appearance comedian who also starred in movies but was still not willing to be saddled with a regular set of partners.

He may not have been quite so clever when it came to realizing that something very new was on the horizon. Television.

In 1947 Paramount Pictures had just got the first television licence ever issued for a commercial station west of the Mississippi. Their problem was that having

Jane Russell, the perfect foil. He always thought she had other attributes, too. From The Paleface, *1948.*

got the licence they didn't know what to do with it. Nor did anyone else for that matter, including Bob Hope, who was convinced that the pictures coming out of that unpleasant-looking tube could never replace radio.

He was even more dubious about the cameras, which were big enough to give a man a hernia merely by looking at them.

The first programme was going to be a variety show featuring all the stars that Paramount could boast – introduced by the funniest of them all, Bob Hope. Mel Shavelson was engaged by the studio head Y. Frank Freeman to write the script for the ninety-minute show. It was such an unusual assignment that Paramount didn't even know what to pay him – no one had ever written a television show before – and settled for a ten-inch black-and-white TV set, which he was allowed to buy wholesale. Strangely, Hope had nothing to do with that deal.

'Bob came out and did his monologue,' said Shavelson, 'to virtual silence from the audience.'

'What's wrong?' he asked his writer. 'Bob,' he replied, 'there's nothing wrong with the jokes. The problem is that you've got a script in your hand.'

'But I've always got a script in my hand,' he protested.

'That's for radio,' Shavelson explained. 'But look around you: there are all these monitors here which people are looking at. They can see you're being paid to read lines that were written for you by somebody else and they resent it.'

It was perhaps the first time that the connection had been made between Hope and his writers, the first occasion when people outside the business realized that he was an actor saying things that he hadn't dreamed up himself.

Shavelson took his courage into both hands and suggested that Bob 'wing it' for the rest of the show – throw his script away and make it look as though he had just thought of the things he said. It was not a particularly happy solution to the problem. 'It turned out to be the biggest clambake of all time. Nobody could remember a line and I don't know how we ever stumbled through it.'

When the show was over, Hope called his writer over. 'Look,' he said, 'this medium of television is never going to catch on. What comedian's going to give up his Sunday golf to memorize a script?'

He could have no idea that before very long even he would see that appearing on TV was more important to him than going on radio – or playing golf. But he would never have to memorize a script. Years later Shavelson told him, 'Because of you they invented the idiot card – and they named it after you.'

From that moment on, the idiot cards – huge white boards on which every line of every joke was laboriously written in thick black letters, like a newsboy's placard – would be an essential part of the act. And soon a gentleman named Barney McNulty became as important a member of the Hope entourage as any of the others who travelled with Bob or appeared on his shows.

McNulty had to sit in on the story conferences, wait for the jokes to be written, to be typed out, listened to by Bob, rejected by Bob, edited by Bob. Then, when they were finally ready, he would have to paint them on to the giant cards, number them – if he got them out of order, the result would be the equivalent of a new California earthquake – and stand with them as close to the cameras as he could get without being seen by the audience. They had to be pretty close since Bob Hope was getting extremely short-sighted. It was a hard job, for not only did Barney have to have wide, strong arms – and he is quite a small man – but required the stamina to be able to run from one end of the stage to the other as Bob turned his head from side to side.

Everyone knew about his cards and the man who carried them. Barney worked on a lot of other TV shows, too (no one in the business could operate the boards quite as well), and enjoyed the joke when Bob mentioned them in his act. For a time Bob talked about the cards even more than he talked about Crosby.

McNulty should not, however, be given all the credit. Being able to read a large card and pretend that it is not there, still more make it sound as though the words came fresh to Bob's mind and not lose any of the timing, is an art in itself. Hope and McNulty made a great team – even if he took a holiday when Bob made his wide-screen films. There was no room for an idiot card on a film sound stage, at least not since John Barrymore had demanded them to help him overcome a drink-sozzled mind which he said was filled with the poetry of Shakespeare. Bob Hope, however, never played Shakespeare.

Barney had to stand right next to the cameraman, 'which in the early days of television made the cameraman extremely nervous because he was expecting to be blundered into at any moment, but we came through as a result of practice.'

It would, however, take a few years before television would become Hope's main medium and Hope TV's most valuable comedy star. For a few years yet, he would do television only when the odd opportunity occurred – and without taking it terribly seriously. How could he be serious when everyone knew that radio was *the* thing? After all, people had had the habit of listening to the big box in the corner of the room for nearly twenty years now. The radio set had replaced the parlour piano. On a winter's evening, people would sit down in front of their fires and listen to Hope telling Colonna that his moustache was a fire risk. 'Professor,' he said to the hairy one, 'did you plant the bomb in the embassy like I told you?'

'Embassy?' said Colonna. 'Great Scot! I thought you said NBC!' It was the sort of stuff Britain's *Goon Show* would revel in ten years later.

Bob could keep his script in front of him for those shows. As Mel Shavelson now recalls, 'The only person who memorized his jokes was Milton Berle – and he also memorized everyone else's, too.' That became as standard a gag as Bob's idiot cards.

Radio was the ideal medium for Hope. But the jokes gave him problems he could not possibly have anticipated in the days before it became so firmly established in the national psyche. Technology had moved on and, thanks to new and – for the times – highly sophisticated recording techniques, now the same show could be broadcast on the East and West coasts, three hours apart. But *The Bob Hope Pepsodent Show* was proving too popular. People living in New York would telephone the jokes they had just heard on the programme to their families and friends in Los Angeles, whose clocks were set three hours earlier. When Bob got to hear of that, he ordered totally different routines for his West Coast listeners, so that no one could beat him to his own punchlines. It was like a radio version of an evening newspaper, always subject to a new edition.

Mel Shavelson recalled, 'In the three hours' time differential, we'd be working right up into broadcast time before we finally had it. In one show, he didn't like what we had done and the show was on the air before we finally came up with a very bad joke that ended the show – and almost ended us.'

Perhaps the best thing of all about radio for Bob was the fact that, scripted jokes or not, he was free to improvise, throwing lines live into the show that none of his writers had planned. The effect on his co-stars was even more disorientating – especially when, much to the stunned amazement of his sponsors, who believed nothing should be allowed to interfere with the literally whiter-than-white image of their product, he indulged his own fancy for off-colour humour.

The prim Dorothy Lamour was a frequent guest on his show. Once, though, she wasn't prepared for a Hope riposte. 'I'll meet you in front of the pawn shop,' the script instructed her to say. Bob was supposed to reply simply, 'OK'. Instead, he replied. 'OK, Dotty. And then you can kiss me under the balls.'

Her shocked, stunned reaction and the collective intake of breath from the audience was drowned by organ music. If nothing else, it proved that Bob Hope could be funny without the help of his writers.

He would not have dared do that on television. He was too tied to what the cue cards said – and he certainly would not have attempted it in the movies. Would *Sorrowful Jones* have been funnier if he hadn't been restricted by the camera angles so carefully worked out by the director Sidney Lanfield? Probably not, because Mel Shavelson was writing it for him and Shavelson knew Hope's mouth from his radio days as well as Bob knew it himself.

This time, he helped him get under the skin of one of Damon Runyon's most colourful characters, the walking racing form in *Little Miss Marker*. If Mel was asked by Bob to punch up a script with new jokes, he was at least working on his own script and there were none of the complications of having to work on someone else's.

There was one other man who was important to Bob Hope at this time, another writer named Barney Dean. Barney was a little man who could make Bob laugh, so much so that he had him put on to the Paramount wages roster – officially as a writer. He was a little bald man who had once been in vaudeville – he called himself 'the world's slowest whirlwind dancer' – and whom Bob had met again, years after those early days. They asked him what he was doing. 'Oh the same thing,' said Barney. 'You know, selling handcuffs.' That was enough to put him on the payroll. All that he wrote was the odd joke, but it was enough for both Bob and Bing, who enjoyed his company for the sake of that company – and the jokes.

It was another one of those good times for Bob Hope movies. *The Great Lover* was made to measure for the familiar Hope character, now so firmly established that no one could conceive of anyone else playing the kind of part that was so much him. The idea of the movie Bob Hope being a great lover seemed patently ridiculous because everyone knew he never got the girl, except in one of the *Road* pictures when he finally does marry Dorothy Lamour and they have a baby – who just happens to be the spitting image of Bing Crosby. (Few people outside the film community had heard much about Hope's reputation with women in Hollywood.)

The Great Lover fostered another Hope image – his own conceit. Every time, in every movie, he was flattered by the leading lady into thinking that she wanted him for his face – and his body. He always fell for it. In this film – in which he played a milksop scoutmaster who just happens to witness a murder – he also fell for Rhonda Fleming, which wasn't a difficult thing to do.

In *Fancy Pants*, in which he played an English butler stranded in the Wild West, he had to fall for Lucille Ball. That was not nearly as easy for him. A man who didn't like sharing jokes with Bing Crosby found it tougher still competing for laughs with

With Lucille Ball in Fancy Pants, *1950.*

the woman who before long would have millions saying that they loved Lucy. But all was well – more than well. It turned into another one of those movies whose titles could well be inscribed below a Bob Hope statue.

The picture was a remake of the classic *Ruggles of Red Gap*, which starred Charles Laughton. Hope's version was better.

He was a busy man. About this time, he made a series of trips to London and discovered that the country of his birth loved him as much as the one that had adopted him all those years before. That went for the King and Queen as much as it did for the men and women who forced their way through the bomb sites and the grime and gloom of postwar Britain to get to his shows. In 1947, he was the star attraction of that year's Royal Command Film Performance at the Odeon, Leicester Square. But it wasn't the only royal command he answered. He and Dolores had just been guests at that month's wedding of Princess (now Queen) Elizabeth and the Duke of Edinburgh. Both events showed that Bob was at the summit of his career – even if he did joke that he was so far away from the main procession that all he saw were 'four white mice pulling a gold-covered snuff box'.

He presented the King with an album of Hollywood stars. The King asked if there was a signed picture of Bing Crosby in it. There was, said Hope. 'But he doesn't write. He just makes three Xs.' 'Why three?' asked the King. 'He has a middle name,' said Bob, who from that moment on was the monarch's favourite star, even if he was closely shadowed by Danny Kaye.

But even royal commands have their problems. Pepsodent refused to accept that a big star like Hope could take time off in the middle of the busiest radio season of the year and threatened to cancel his contract for the next year. He still went – and broadcast his monologue live from London. Hope wasn't about to cheat his audience. It was one thing recording the sketches and other dateless parts of the show, which he did, but there was no way in which he would endanger the topicality of the main part of his routine.

Hope's answer to all that was to make sure that he had the last laugh. He didn't allow Pepsodent to consider sacking him. Instead, he switched what was now *The Bob Hope Show* to new sponsors, Swan Soap.

Hope's jokes were as funny as ever, aided by a new writer called Larry Gelbart, later to confirm his talent on *The Sid Caesar Show* and, much more significantly, with *M*A*S*H*.

The format wasn't very different from the Pepsodent programme, with the exception of the fact that he now had a new regular girl singer, a twenty-five-year-old named Doris Day.

She was expected to do a lot, although she wouldn't even have contemplated doing one thing that might have been expected of her. Part of her role in the new show was taking part in comedy sketches with Hope. In one, she wondered why, when Bob was at the Palm Springs Racquet Club, he didn't take an expensive suite like Clark Gable or Van Johnson. Why did she want to know? ' Well,' she said, 'sooner or later they're going to find out that you're living under the kitchen window in a wigwam!'

He might have been glad that Day restricted her contacts with Hope to the radio studio. There was enough trouble coming his way from Dolores. A disgruntled employee rang Mrs Hope with the vital news that her husband was at that very moment in bed with an attractive blonde.

There were more personal appearances now, more occasions when for a usually undisclosed sum – payable by all except the charities to whom he performed more often than his usual audiences imagined – he could plug his occasional new television shows. However, he wouldn't yet forsake radio for a full-time TV career. He was going to see how well Milton Berle, the first to sign up for the box, did first.

When he would do television, he still had the perfect band to back him – Les Brown, or Les Brown and the Band of Renown, as his outfit came to be known. He would be Bob's orchestra for the rest of his career. There was no doubt, however, that Bob was the boss. 'Oh yes,' Brown told me. '[If a producer got difficult], we'd always say, "You're not the producer, Bob is".'

But he never overestimated Hope's singing ability, although not a show went on air without his performing a song – and to most people's ears very nicely too. 'His singing was adequate, and his delivery was fine. But he just didn't have the voice of Sinatra, Tony Bennett or Nat "King" Cole.'

Brown became a fixture of the radio programme as much as did Jerry Colonna and Frances Langford. When television did seem an overpowering temptation, the musician would be ready for it. The few people who had sets would have loved Bob's jokes as much as anyone else. Possibly even as much as Harry S. Truman. When the President so unexpectedly beat Governor Thomas Dewey of New York in 1948, Bob sent him a telegram. It said simply, 'UNPACK'. Truman liked it so much, he had the wire framed.

Bob himself was more interested in the kind of documents that he filed away in either his personal safe or one at the bank – the sort that proclaimed the number of shares or other business interests in which he was involved. These were by far the most profitable part of the partnership with Crosby. Not only did they have their oil interests – when Bob sold one field, he alone netted $3.5 million, a vast fortune in the early 1950s – another liquid was to be an equally good investment. He and Bing put money into the then new product, Minute Maid Orange Juice – and did themselves rather more good than had they merely taken in the vitamins. The chances of either of them actually drinking orange juice for other than publicity purposes were, of course, rather remote.

But Bob would for years after admit, 'We meshed and we made a nice dollar together.' There was no doubt, however, about the bond that existed between the two men. 'The chemistry was remarkable. They complemented each other beautifully,' remembers Les Brown. 'Whenever Bing was announced on the radio and it was published that he was coming on our show, the ratings went sky high. Later, on television, it was just the same – which is why Bing was the most frequent guest we had on both radio and TV.'

Not that ratings were ever low. It got to be one of the things that Hope was taking for granted. Then, just as he might have been forgiven for thinking that life was getting a little dull, the People's Republic of North Korea came to his aid – and invaded the South. The crossing of the 38th Parallel meant that his favourite audience was ready for him once again.

In fur-trimmed hat and battledress coat, he boarded a plane in the United States and got off some time the next day in the snowy wastes of Korea. The soldiers, airmen and Marines welcomed him and his party much as they would an unexpected food parcel. They waited and cheered – no matter what guns were firing and how bad the weather. The group were equally prepared to accept whatever was thrown at them.

Once, the helicopter in which they were travelling developed engine trouble and all the troupe were thrown to the ground in the course of the crash landing.

Dolores with children Linda and Tony, in London 1961.

Janis Paige, then on the threshold of a movie career of her own, told me she was dragged out of the craft in the midst of a blizzard, forced to trudge in the snow and taken to a hut. 'We were a thousand miles from nowhere. I was in a hut and safe, but, looking back on what could have happened to us it could have been much more serious.'

It turned out that the engine, engulfed in driving snow, had cut out and the helicopter had had to 'float' down.

Despite it all, Bob Hope couldn't have been happier. Frances Langford and Jerry Colonna were also with him once again. Lana Turner came too, and there was also the finest assortment of starlets who never saw a movie camera. It was the perfect opportunity to play to his favourite audience – and a great excuse to leave Dolores behind. (He used to joke that, when she attended one of the many showbiz tributes he received, it was the first time she found out what he did for a living. 'She probably thought I was a test pilot for United Airlines'.) *bh*

Chapter Eight – WHERE THERE'S LIFE

There were again the right stories for the right locale. The Red Chinese were joining the fight on the side of the North Koreans. We read it in the papers, heard it on the radio, but knew it for sure because Bob Hope had a joke ready for the occasion: 'I know this is Korea because, when you send your laundry out here, it comes back with a fortune cookie in it.'

His fortune, his good fortune, was that the younger brothers, if not the sons, of the men he had been playing to in World War Two wanted him as much as the older men ever did. In places like Puson, Wonsan, Pyonjang and the capital, Seoul he told jokes that were suitable for the newsreels and radio shows he was recording at the same time, and several about the breasts and bottoms of the women who came with him that were distinctly not suitable. Again, there were certain ladies who had to pass the usual Hope auditions, which were not limited to their thespian talents.

The army didn't worry about that, or, if they did, they were ready to bypass it, prepare another letter of commendation and organize the next show in an army base one day, a makeshift airfield the next, or perhaps on the deck of an aircraft carrier or a warship the day after.

It may be difficult all these years later to imagine just what it was to attend a show of the kind the Hope travelling circus offered. The troops, thousands of them, loved every minute. In peacetime there would never have been an audience like it, before Woodstock and the rallies for the Beatles moved in on the territory. Mostly, they were gathered together in vast open-air stadiums, usually sitting on the ground, their guns at the ready. They presented the biggest sitting target in any of the combat zones: an air reconnaissance flight could easily have pinpointed a huge concentration of troops who were not exactly in a position to get up and start firing.

Their faces were frequently grimy. They were all desperately tired – the ones picked to attend the shows were those who had just come off duty. They were equally frustrated. The sight of a curvy girl not wearing a great deal sent them wild, even more wild than Bob Hope's jokes, but, since Bob Hope was the star, he knew when enough was enough and when the time had come to get in on his own act. But he told the stories about the girls just the same. He knew that was what the guys wanted to hear. When the ladies of the Hope chorus arrived, 'the wolf whistles blew three planes off the runway,' he was to say.

He liked to tell the story of the woman he met in Australia. 'It started to rain and

Vaudeville again. A publicity still from Road To Bali.

she took her dress and held it over her hat. 'I said, "What are you doing that for? Your legs are getting all wet." And she said, "The hat's brand-new. My legs are fifty years old".'

Jerry Colonna was always there. All he had to do was open his mouth, let out his trademark roar, and the effect on the stadium where the show was being played was not very different from that of a mortar shell being lobbed. It certainly made enough noise. The place erupted – into cheers and laughs.

Janis Paige did a musical number on her own, then one with Bob, and usually ended up doing a soft-shoe routine. 'The role of the women on the tour was to be beautiful and sexy and fun and be looked at,' she told me. But she never felt she was just a sex object. It was an experience to treasure – a dangerous one at that.

'You don't realize how dangerous it is until you get home and begin to look back and realize the places we've been.'

There was something in that for the troops – to know that civilians, and some of them female civilians, had put themselves in danger to entertain them. What that did for their fighting abilities hasn't to date been recorded, as far as I know, in any official history of the war.

Janis Paige remembers Hope as 'a gentleman'. She said, 'I never heard him use a cuss word, the kind of language you hear today.'

Bob's relationship with some of the women who were around him at the time has, however, been offered to history. Barbara Payton, an actress who was best known for various performances in famous men's beds, told *Confidential* magazine about her relationship with Hope. She said they met in Dallas and got on well enough to take things further. 'We only knew each other a few hours before we knew each other as well as a boy and girl ever can.' It was the beginning of a steamy affair, during which Bob furnished his mistress with a luxury apartment of her own. Bob didn't merely use it for his lovemaking. One morning he was spotted on the balcony of the flat – wearing an apron and sweeping the floor. Such was the power of love and lust. (It is interesting that *Confidential* ran that article about the Hope–Payton relationship. Arthur Marx told me, 'I think he's pretty powerful. A friend of mine who was publisher of *Confidential* – before all the tabloids – told me that Hope was actually able to stop something that was in the magazine.')

Barbara Payton even gave up a career of her own (she was contracted to Universal) to be with Hope, not always discreetly. There were no morals patrols out for him, at least none that Dolores could summon. On the other hand, the vice squad did move in on his Toluca Lake home – to stop a raffle being held as part of a garden party organized by Dolores (always the religious one) – in aid of a monastery.

She quite possibly would have wanted to put Bob in such an establishment.

Once Payton was out of the way – Bob tired easily of some women, especially when he knew that there was always another one on the way – he moved on.

With Marilyn Maxwell - the real love in his life.

This time, the 'other' one was Marilyn Maxwell, who left no room at all for any competition. Maxwell was one of those actresses whom studio press releases liked to describe as a platinum blonde. In those days when even press agents had to be careful about what they said, they would have gloried in printing her picture, but would have been reluctant to put into words precise details of her attributes. She was not just curvy, but had a bust that would have sent a sculptor into paroxysms of delight – the precise effect she had on Bob Hope. Her face was more beautiful than any he had seen. She was also a superb lover – which was why Frank Sinatra had had his own passionate affair with her (much to the disgust of Mrs Nancy Sinatra, who discovered that the diamond bracelet she found in his car and thought was coming to her for a New Year's Eve present was actually intended for Marilyn).

Hope was smitten as he had never been before. She travelled to England with him. She went with him to Japan and then on to Korea. They were infatuated with each other – so much so that their love even survived a confrontation at the

Jayne Mansfield was just his cup of coffee (1957). In England, Diana Dors was just his cup of tea (1956).

apartment he had bought her. That was the night Bob arrived unexpectedly, shouted out, 'It's me, Bob "Great Lover" Hope' – and discovered not just Maxwell in a state of undress, but Jimmy Durante wearing little more than his shorts.

Durante was known for many things – including hooking nose-to-nose with Bob on a radio programme and singing with him (it passed for singing) 'The Gentlemen With The Proboscis' – but being a lover was not one of them. Hope didn't know whether to be more amused than annoyed when he saw Durante in the polka-dot shorts walk out of a closet.

Everyone knew of the Hope–Maxwell affair. Dolores certainly did. He claimed that his wife's Catholic upbringing would never have allowed her to consider a divorce, although he had asked for one. That did not mean that Dolores didn't threaten a divorce – at a time when she knew it would be inconvenient (and expensive) for him to go along with the idea.

Marilyn sailed on the *Queen Mary* with Bob for another command performance for the King and Queen. On board, Hope received a telegram from Dolores warning him that, unless he ended the affair, she would demand a divorce. Bob himself didn't want to go down that route, but he always told his mistress that it was Dolores who presented the real stumbling block. For a time, Marilyn seemed to accept that. They went everywhere together on private nights out as well as professionally. If she had to be out of town, Bob found a way to be with her.

She even wore what looked like a wedding ring on the appropriate finger after she finally divorced the man to whom she had really been married, Andy McIntyre. It got to the stage where people were calling her 'Mrs Hope' and without protest from either of them.

Maxwell co-starred with him in his second foray into the world of Damon Runyon, *The Lemon Drop Kid* (hit song: 'Silver Bells', which was originally written as 'Tinkle Bells' until someone pointed out that the word 'tinkle' could have had a double meaning). Starring with Marilyn showed how strong the love was. Bob still had the power to choose his cast as much as he had the ability to select the scripts on which he worked. She was the only Hope mistress to be either good enough to get her billing under his, which might be considered to be highly appropriate, or to be given the chance to do so.

She could get practically anything she wanted from him while she granted similar favours herself. The only thing he still resolutely wouldn't do for her was divorce Dolores, although by all accounts he kept promising it.

In Korea, she was fêted as a star almost as much as was Bob himself – with his full approval. Others on the tour had never seen that before. Hope was jealous of his role as the head guy in the party and didn't lightly surrender that status, as Jerry Colonna and the others could testify.

The fact that he left alone every other woman on the tour showed how serious he was with and about Marilyn. (Gloria De Haven, who had been part of the original party, left for home when she discovered that Maxwell was around for more than the ride.)

She went with him when Hope was entertained by General Douglas MacArthur in Tokyo, a place that Bob had wanted to visit for some time, so that he could plug the local showings of *The Lemon Drop Kid*. The general, who before long would be fired by President Truman for trying to take the war into China itself – a sentiment Bob backed to the hilt – welcomed him as he would a war hero (even though he felt that he himself was the only real hero around).

Hope had particularly endeared himself to MacArthur by phoning him on the day that the North Koreans invaded. The General knew that Hope wanted to entertain. He also knew that Bob was fast developing a reputation as the prize hawk of Hollywood, although the term had not yet come into frequent use.

He was enthusiastic to the point of painting the lily. He and Marilyn flew into Wonsan one day and found that they had arrived even before the American troops had landed. US Marines had been scheduled to take the town, but the South Koreans had done the job for them a couple of days earlier. So the entertainers waited patiently and then, eventually, the Marines arrived. One man was quoted as saying, 'The only thing we're going in here for is to give Bob Hope an audience.' That audience was always going to be special for him. As Les Brown told me, 'I'd announce Bob Hope and we'd play "Thanks For The Memory". He would come on and, when he walked out, he'd start as we cut down [the music]. The applause came the moment he said, "Good afternoon" – the crowd would start laughing.'

Having Marilyn Maxwell along boosted more than just the show in which she played. He was comforted to know that she was there. The affair came to an end only when Marilyn realized that there was no chance of her really becoming Mrs Hope. Bob was genuinely distraught. Every now and again, they found reason to be together again, right until 1954 when Marilyn finally married.

There was always something to cheer Bob up, however – if it meant lots of applause and an equal amount of money. Both came to him in spades when he finally agreed that maybe appearing on his own TV programme would be more worthwhile than just playing golf. He might have been drawn to that conclusion by something that happened on the golf course – using a number-three iron in an exhibition at St Louis. A little girl ran into his path just as the ball left his club and he hit her on the head. 'She went down and I had the next eighteen hours of torture until I found that she was OK.'

If Marilyn had been with him, he might have had that torture eased. As it was, according to Bob Slatzer, when he went back to Korea, an advance party of women were there waiting for him. 'These were not stars or girls who worked in the shows,' he explained, 'they were the ones who hung around the set, usually beauty-contest winners.'

They knew what Bob wanted them for, but, if he asked them to go anywhere, they ran. There had even been a set of twins whom Crosby and Hope shared. When neither Bing nor Bob were in Hollywood, they happily volunteered for 'service' in Korea. When Hope got back, they were waiting with him at the radio or TV studio.

He had made his first TV show, for Frigidaire, in April 1950. He wasn't intending to do television instead of radio. At first, the routine never varied. There was radio every week and television once a month. Radio remained his favourite. He still regarded it as the 'grown-up' medium, but matters were taken out of his hands when Lever Brothers, who had sponsored his programmes, were concerned both with falling ratings and the fact that Bob seemed to be on the road more than he was at home and available to get to the Hollywood studios of NBC.

The television shows were a great success, with Jane Russell on hand as regular guest star. Everyone expected, once that triumph had been confirmed with a second show, that Bob would now have a weekly outing on the tube like Milton Berle. Les Brown thought so, too. In fact, so did Bob.

'He was in New York, staying at the Hampshire House, and I called him about something,' Brown told me. 'He said, "Les, you know, I had my pen in my hand and I was going to sign up for a weekly television show. But something is wrong. I'll be overexposed. So I put the pen down and said no." Well, that cost me a lot of money. I'd have been better off if he had a weekly show. But he said that nine shows a year was enough for his kind of stuff and he was right.'

That was the official reason – that he thought there would be too much pressure on him to be fresh, week in, week out. The unofficial reason was that he needed those trips out of town to be with those women. Now there would be a series of Bob Hope TV specials – so that every show would indeed seem special. If they happened only once every so often, sometimes only every three months, he reasoned, people would want him all the more. At first, he aired his show at monthly intervals. It was more work for the writers, whose jokes and scripts – the original gags typed on the original paper – were by now being stored alphabetically and under subject titles in a vault attached to the Toluca Lake house. This was a huge walk-in safe controlled by a combination lock. By the time he did his last NBC TV show there would be close to eight million of those jokes lining the shelves of the vault.

He would say again and again how much he needed those writers. 'The only reason I was a hit,' he has said, 'was because I had the best group of writers ever assembled.'

Yet, according to Arthur Marx, they were treated like slave labour. 'He had contracts where there would be nominal money involved and he'd have young writers whom he'd put on. He was very good about hiring young writers and giving them a chance. But he'd hire them, sign them to a three-year contract with options at the end of every year. And he'd never let them know if he was going to keep them on until after the season was over – by which time it was too late for them to get another job if he weren't going to hire them back. That's slave labour.'

But, with the dawn of his television career, the writers felt as much for him as they did for themselves. *They* only had to do what they had been doing for years, while Hope had to face an entirely different medium and they saw that for the first time he looked and sounded nervous. But he did well, better than he could have imagined, partly because the people watching the programmes loved everything they saw. If the only competition was the test card, he couldn't fail. He didn't.

Technology was the one thing that got in the way. The show was broadcast from New York and there was no way of transmitting television the 3,000 miles that separated the East from the West Coast. The only solution to the problem was to do the shows live for audiences east of the Rockies and send a 'kinescope' recording to the NBC stations in the west. TV recordings were pretty bad in those days – they were movies shot by cameras focused directly on to the TV tube – but even the audiences who saw these decided they liked them enough to want more. 'He was,' said Les Brown, 'the only guy who could walk down Hollywood Boulevard or down Vine Street and everything stopped. He'd sign autographs. He just loved that kind of thing.'

Hope wanted more, too, although he realized – and said so publicly – that television was a minority interest. 'It's amazing,' he said, 'how many people see you on TV. I did my first television show a month ago and the next day five million television sets were sold. The people who couldn't sell theirs threw them away.'

It was obvious from the start that Hope and TV were made for each other. It was equally obvious that comedy was made for television. Hope's built-in detection system (he had had it since before radar was invented) told him that inviting other comics on to his shows would only increase the popularity of the programmes. He usually got the biggest laughs himself – and not always at the expense of his guests.

He was also now following the pattern he had adopted in his army shows – giving 'chances' to girls whose talents were usually confined to their hip and bust measurements. One of these was a pin-up girl called Jeanne Carmen. Jeanne to this day proudly shows covers of the magazines for which she posed and photographs they included which display her in what today would be considered extremely decorous attitudes. In those days they were daring beyond belief – but she rarely showed a nipple. To Bob Hope, however, she was more generous.

She was also a very good golfer, which was how Bob came to meet her in the first place. Her speciality was as a 'trick-shot golfer', getting golf balls into the hole using amazing contortions to do so. She appeared on the Hope TV show – and fluffed her lines. But they weren't the lines Bob was interested in. 'I understand you're a great golfer,' he said. She acknowledged that she was – and set up a golfing date with him for the following day.

'I didn't realize that Bob was interested in more than my golf because I was eighteen, nearly nineteen, and very naïve, and I thought, Gosh! This is great.' They played and she discovered he wasn't quite the golfer he thought he was. 'He always said his handicap was a lot better than it really was and the only way he could win was to exaggerate it. He was absolutely adamant about winning. He loved to win.'

Soon after that, she realized what his intentions really were. They had a date at the Waldorf Astoria. She was at the table first. He came in afterwards – with an entourage. Bob was flustered – and arranged for someone else to sit with her, 'a beard', which she at the time thought was just what men grew on their faces. She found out that night. 'Actually, I guess he had no intentions of going to dinner with me. I guess it was upstairs that I was supposed to be having the dinner. Nevertheless, I got a good dinner.'

The affair was surprisingly open. He took her all over the country with him and, if photographers snapped them together, he didn't seem to mind. 'He used to call me all the time. If I was in New York, I'd call him in California. I'd reverse the charges. Sometimes the operator would say, "Do you mean Bob Hope the comedian?" and I'd say, "No, Bob Hope the plumber".'

There was no confusion over which Bob Hope she meant when they were

Marlon Brando meets his match. But then he hasn't been a Godfather yet (at the Oscars, 1955).

playing golf one day with two surprising partners – the Duke and Duchess of Windsor. He was not in the least in awe of the former British King and nor was she. Bob didn't even mind introducing her. That evening, Hope and his girlfriend and the Duke and Duchess of Windsor drank pink champagne together and then sat at the same table for dinner. No one bothered with them, she said. Not even when she said the champagne got to her and she became, as she admitted to me, 'really stupid and nasty'. Hope 'said something I didn't like and I said "Go to hell" and I jumped up and turned the table almost over and walked across the dance floor. Bob actually came up to the room and said, "Please, honey, come back. In this business, you have to be nice, to be sweet to people." He was always like that, always good, always sweet, always nice.'

He was nice to her when they made love in Hope's bed in the house at Toluca Lake. She claims she didn't even realize he was married. She might have been more honest if she said she appreciated that he was married to his work.

Bob was approaching his fiftieth birthday, which some considered old at the time, but he was working as though his life depended on it – which in a way it did.

He was working at finding new money deals – like the one that gave him a small

He was always the chief. So he bought the team.

financial interest in his home-town baseball team, the Cleveland Indians. That, of course, gave rise to suggestions that he was really only interested in beating Crosby at his own game – Bing was the man behind the Pittsburgh Pirates.

But these were just diversions. Once the Korean war was established as just another theatre for him to visit, he had to find ways of filling in the time between his trips to the peninsula and the ones to the NBC TV studios. He was still firmly of the belief that he had to get back to the movie studio and make as many films as his writers could churn out. There was no more shortage of material than there was of celluloid to thread through the cameras.

After *The Lemon Drop Kid*, he was back to the *My Favourite* series, this time *My Favourite Spy*, in which he co-starred (even if he might not have liked the term) with the always beautiful Hedy Lamarr. It was the last of the series, if the first to specify Bob's usual occupation in the title. This time he was playing the double of an international agent, one brave, the other ... well, the way Bob Hope always was in films. It wasn't the best film he ever made.

The picture was directed by Hal Kanter, who had been working for Crosby for years. 'Maybe,' he told me, 'that's how I got to work for Bob.' He wasn't the only one to notice that, whatever it was that Bing Crosby had, Bob Hope wanted, too.

Nevertheless, he liked Hope a lot more than Crosby. 'Bing was a strange man. He was reasonably generous about his time and about his work. But he was very, very cold and aloof. Much more than Bob.'

The title of *Son of Paleface* said it all – a sequel the way almost every sequel was dubbed in those days. (Today they would just say *Paleface 2* and it wouldn't be any better for it.)

It was the old idea of cashing in on a success and making it a failure. Jane Russell again looked stunning and Roy Rogers and Trigger looked distinctly uncomfortable, which seems to have gone for the audience, too. But better things were on the way. Or should that be on the road? This time, *The Road to Bali*. It was in many ways the last of the traditional *Road* films, although another one would come nine years later.

Again Dorothy Lamour sat between the two men, virtually either ignored or treated as a punchbag by them, according to Hal Kanter, but she and Bing and Bob were all looking older and that went for the sets, too. The first of the series in colour only seemed to emphasize that the South Seas had never seen the scenery used and the men who designed it had never seen the location either. The gags were of the strictly I've-heard-that-one-before variety and the wonder was that Bob Hope of all people, the great editor, allowed them to pass his lips. But it was a pleasant enough diversion. As for the two male stars, the main interest as usual was the money.

But neither depended on the *Road* for his income and they both had plans for the near future. Bob's next venture was a little better – one of his last public outings with Marilyn Maxwell, who, it was now revealed, was so short-sighted that she could see practically nothing at times. 'She was as near-sighted as hell,' says Hal Kanter, who directed the new picture, 'as near-sighted as Mr Magoo, but a lot prettier.' The film was called *Off Limits*, which didn't apply to the audience, although not as many people as in the past lined up for a Bob Hope picture. Was this the writing on the wall? ⓑ

Chapter Nine – THE GREAT LOVER

He called his next venture *Here Come The Girls*. The title said more about Bob Hope than about the picture, which was set in the 1890s. It told the old – by now old, old – story of the coward who thinks he has become a hero, the chorus boy who is flattered into being turned into a star. Of course he is neither of these things, but, when he accidentally traps a murderer, there are people who have reasons to keep the flattery going.

The title of the movie after that, *Casanova's Big Night* – it was to be the last big-budgeted Bob Hope costume vehicle – was also singularly appropriate for Hope. He was increasing his Casanova-like activities to an extent that would have done credit to the film's amorous Venetian eponym. The character, in one classic scene, regrets how he has to curtail his attentions to the ladies round about. 'I can only work two canals at a time,' he says.

Hal Kanter, who had also directed *Off Limits*, was in charge of this movie, too. Bob got a 'little impatient ' at his direction, he recalled. 'He called me aside and said, "Please just do it. Don't let's analyse it, let's just do it".' But, he said, Bob enjoyed the idea of costume parts – an enjoyment he demonstrated in countless television specials. 'He would very often find any reason to put on a costume, and the more outrageous the costume the better.'

Part of the reason for his impatience was that he had to get back to the golf course. There was always something to do. 'We used to call him "Rapid Robert",' said Kanter.

Rapid Robert had to bid for the company of Joan Fontaine, who was making a rare excursion into comedy. 'They got on beautifully,' says Kanter. 'She had a wonderful sense of humour, and a very bawdy sense of humour at that, a very funny lady.'

She, too, was forbidden territory for Hope, but there continued to be so many other women in his life that he wouldn't have worried about it. He kept women in apartments all over Los Angeles. It was the duty of his brother George to deliver the rent money to the young ladies, a job he did assiduously until Mrs George Hope found him in a compromising situation with a particularly beautiful girl. From then on, he had to be careful – and asked Bob Slatzer to take on the errand for him. Slatzer liked it, too, he told me. All he had to do was knock on a door and see a very pretty, shapely girl open it, smile and take the money.

Once, though, it went wrong. Dolores had taken a call from the girl's landlord. He hadn't received the currently owed money – which Slatzer had claimed to have

10105-2/67

A slight case of Gorilla Warfare (from Here Come The Girls, *1953).*

delivered. Naturally, Dolores wanted to know what it was all about, and Bob had difficulty in telling her. Eventually, she was persuaded that it had something to do with just one of her husband's many real-estate deals. But George wanted to know why Slatzer had let him down, although that wasn't the phrase he used. 'You spent it on some broad?' he asked.

Eventually, the girl admitted she had used the money to buy clothes and the affair blew over, as did her relationship with Bob.

There were so many of these girls, Bob's business associates maintain, that it was difficult to keep track of them or know which one went where. When he went to the London Palladium for the first time in 1951, there were a number hovering in the background as always.

The Palladium always served as a kind of Mecca for Hope, as for most other American stars. Danny Kaye had made it virtually his own territory in 1947 and, as a result, every subsequent performer there wanted to show they could do equally well at the theatre. Few managed it, but week in, week out, a top transatlantic personality headed the bill.

Lew Grade, who at the time was responsible for booking the Palladium acts, had been trying for a long time to get Bob to come. Eventually, he flew to California to persuade him. He was given the gold-star treatment when he arrived at Paramount and was shown into Hope's dressing room.

Sitting there, too, was an English clergyman. When Bob came in, he welcomed Grade. He knew what the impressario wanted. Then he asked, 'Do you know the Reverend Butterworth?'

The man who is now Lord Grade of Elstree had to say that he did not. Hope explained that the priest ran a boys' club in London's Camberwell. 'I'll come to the theatre,' he said, 'providing you give my fee to Clubland.'

The Sunday evening show in November 1951 was a sensation. In October the following year, he did tremendous business for a fortnight in the company of one of the sexiest women singers in Britain. She went under the stage name of Yana. Her theme song was 'Climb Up The Wall', which apparently Bob did, figuratively speaking. He was also photographed peering down the explosive cleavage of another TV personality named Sabrina (it was apparently sexy in fifties Britain to have only one name).

From that moment on the Palladium was his London home. He went back again and again. He appeared there at Royal Variety Shows, too. At one, he and Judy Garland did an act together.

'I'm serious, Bob,' said Judy. 'I have quite a problem and I want to ask you a big favour.'

'Well. sure, Jude. What is it?'

'Well, I know you're with Paramount, Bob, but I'm making a musical for MGM and I need a new leading man. He must be very good-looking, tremendously

Bob in his element.

talented, have loads of appeal to women. So naturally, I thought of you.'

'Well, gee thanks,' said Bob, salivating.

'Yes,' she said. 'I'm sure you could recommend someone.'

Then insult was piled on injury. Her choice had narrowed to two men – Bing Crosby and Frank Sinatra.

'Well,' he said, 'that's one and a half men, and I'm not sure which is the half.'

To help him out, Bing appeared from the wings and Hope and Crosby were together again with a new leading lady in the middle.

The royal shows were, in their way, the grander British equivalents of the tributes American entertainment organizations like the Friars Club like to award their top personalities – an accolade that can't be bought or lobbied for. When the Friars in New York gave Bob a testimonial dinner attended by some of the top men in the land, he feigned modesty: 'No one can be this great,' he said, 'but you've finally convinced me.' Then he added: 'If I'd known you were going to eulogise me like this, I'd have done the decent thing and died first.'

Millions of people were grateful that he had not.

But was Bing Crosby? To everyone's amazement, Crosby was not at the dinner, even though he had not only been invited, but there was an empty seat reserved for him next to Bob's own throughout the evening. 'I never go to those things,' he protested afterwards. But it set a great number of Hollywood tongues wagging.

'Bob was deeply hurt,' said Bob Slatzer. 'He would never have failed to turn up for an affair that honoured Bing. There was a great dislike that he developed for Bing after that. I think it was the fact that he might have been a little bit jealous.' It might, however, have been the first public confirmation of something that people close to them knew only too well – the pair who before long would sing a duet called 'Teamwork' were not as close as they liked their public to think.

Hurt he was, extraordinarily hurt. Yet he valued the on-stage friendship, which he hoped was still there, and he certainly continued to value Bing's pulling power on his programme. So any private hurt was publicly covered up.

And he had a lot to be grateful for. The awards continued to multiply and now, at last, he had an Oscar of sorts to put on his sideboard. He didn't get it for a movie part, but as a special award for his services to the industry; it was a decent consolation prize.

For her part, Dolores worried about certain other consolations in his life. Jan King was to tell *The Globe* about Bob's sexual antics, which she said only once involved her personally – he made a serious pass at her in his trophy room the day that she first reported to work as his secretary.

'It was just a kind of thing that happens,' she would explain to me in the autumn of 1997, six years after the magazine articles appeared. Arthur Marx says she told him she had decided to stay in Hope's employ after that because 'I was just testing him. But I figured, if I'm going to have to shack up with him and take dictation at a hundred and fifty words a minute, I'm not going to do it for any price. So I just told him, "You're a married man" and ... he just zipped his pants back up and we went back to the trophy room. I got off the casting couch. And then we had a good understanding after.'

But there is no doubt that she saw what went on in Hope's love life from that time onwards.

Arthur Marx quoted her as saying that he was a 'lecher'. 'That was entirely untrue,' she protested to me. She said she spoke to *The Globe* because she had financial problems and that they misquoted her. 'He was always very kind and considerate,' she remembers. Yet she was quoted as saying that 'talent scouts' all over Hollywood brought him women at his command.

She talked in the article of his buying a house in Palm Springs, which he had decorated by a designer, with whom he then had a passionate affair that lasted six years. He used the house simply as a love nest which Dolores almost never visited. 'She never just popped in on him down at the desert for fear of what she would find.'

None of those stories appeared in any of the many books which Bob himself now wrote, or at least on which he had his name, books with titles like *This Is On Me*; *Have Tux, Will Travel* and *Don't Shoot, It's Only Me.* They were all written in partnership with ghost writers, the last of them with Mel Shavelson, who did have equal billing on the cover. As far as Hope was concerned, writing was just another branch of showbusiness.

So what else was new? Anyone wanting to ask what made Rapid Robert run had to ask himself that question continually – because Hope was constantly inventing new things to do. Like Don Quixote, he was in the midst of an eternal quest, although he chose more sensible idols to knock down than mere windmills.

If he looked to his past, the shows to the troops had to be the things of which he was most proud. So why not do them again? It wasn't his fault that America didn't have a war to fight at the time. That was why he went to Greenland in 1954. There were still American troops there and they were dreaming of a white Christmas that all of them would rather see at home.

General 'Rosie' ODonnell, their commander, thought he had the answer for these soldiers huddled in the icy wastes of the Thule base. Why not ask Bob to come over and entertain them? It was like Santa Claus coming alive, knocking on Hope's door and telling him he had a sleigh waiting for a journey to paradise.

He jumped at the idea and so did a whole group of other entertainers who decided that it wouldn't be a bad idea to reprise their World War Two and Korea glories. Les Brown was there with his band; so was Colonna. And so were the girls – new sex symbols like Anita Ekberg and Jayne Mansfield.

Sometimes it was difficult, especially when his gags had to compete with Jayne, whom he constantly encouraged to bend over – in his direction. Both he and his audience knew very quickly that she didn't believe in wearing any underwear.

It would be the way that Bob would spend Christmas for decades afterwards. Dolores didn't object. She may or may not have thought about what Bob was going to get up to when he was away with all those pretty girls – and, rest assured *that* was precisely what he would get up to – but she reconciled herself to the thought that he was doing his duty and by giving him up to the country at this most family-centred holiday, she was doing her duty, too.

The routine would follow every year after that. The family would have a Christmas dinner, with the giving of presents, a few days before he left for a service base somewhere overseas and then a wonderful New Year's Eve together when he got back.

Bob Hope had found a way of having his war and enjoying it, too – even when there wasn't any fighting going on. Later, when things did get tough again, he was to be in his element. For the moment, however, he returned from the front with more peaceful things to do.

His next movie. *The Seven Little Foys*, written and directed by Mel Shavelson. 'I thought it would be a perfect vehicle for Bob. It was the story of a vaudevillian and gave Bob a chance to both be himself and to go back to his own early days in vaudeville,' Mel told me.

BOB HOPE

James Cagney in his favourite pose as a song-and-dance man. With Bob in The Seven Little Foys.

It was the first time he had ever played a real person. Eddie Foy was a comedian – which meant that Bob could be funny – who, when his wife left him with their seven children, decided that the only way he could look after them and still try to earn a living was to take all the kids on to the stage and into a family act.

It was also the first time that Bob had tried to imitate anyone. Of all his characteristics and talents, imitations are not his bag. He is too much of an original. He is a terrible impressionist and cannot do dialects. At first, he tried to imitate Eddie Foy's habit of wiping the saliva from the corner of his mouth every time he spoke. Before long, he dropped the attempt. 'He couldn't tell the jokes properly,' said Shavelson. 'he was thinking of the mouth too much.'

It all worked splendidly, especially the one scene in which James Cagney reprised his old part of George M. Cohan from *Yankee Doodle Dandy* and danced on a table top with Hope. Cagney was brilliant. 'I've got my tap shoes in the car,' he said the day he turned up for work – and then wouldn't take a cent for a job that was a labour of love. Mel asked him why not: 'Because, when I was struggling in vaudeville, I could always get a square meal at the Foys' house.'

You knew how good *The Seven Little Foys* really was by just how bad Hope's next film would be. In *That Certain Feeling* he played a cartoonist, but the whole thing was really a cartoon of himself, a parody. The uncertain feeling you had after watching it was to ask if Bob Hope had had his day.

He tried to resurrect his prospects with new films on the agenda, but the two movies that followed both went up like lead balloons. The 1956 movie *The Iron Petticoat* had a Cold War setting and he was lucky that a heated-up war didn't overtake him with angry fans demanding their money back.

It achieved the impossible – turning a film starring not just Hope but also Katharine Hepburn into the biggest flop either had ever had. On the surface, it was another *Ninotchka* – a year before the exquisite *Silk Stockings*, the Fred Astaire–Cyd Charisse musical remake of the original Garbo *Ninotchka*. A US Air Force officer (Hope) persuades a Russian aviatrix to defect to the West. But it worked not at all.

Something big and important was needed to redeem his reputation. It came with another biopic, also written (with Jack Rose) and directed by Mel Shavelson. *Beau James* was probably the best thing he ever did, but the desperately sought Oscar still eluded him. The story of the crooked but lovable James J. Walker, Mayor of New York in the 1930s, was an ideal medium with which Bob Hope could prove what some people had suspected all along. He was a very good actor, very good indeed. There was, of course, a love interest in the picture (Vera Miles) and because His Honour (or rather Hizonnah) liked to crack jokes there were plenty of opportunities for Hope one-liners.

There should have been more movies like that, the middle-aged Bob Hope needed to express himself on all cylinders, and though he may not have known it – and you have to seriously ask yourself whether he did know it – acting was one of the strongest of them that he possessed.

Yet neither this movie nor *The Seven Little Foys* gets the recognition these days it deserves. 'I resent the fact that they are completely overlooked today,' says Mel Shavelson. *Paris Holiday*, which followed later that year, was not nearly as effective, although it did co-star the comedian Fernandel, who was inevitably billed as the French Bob Hope. They seem to have spent a great deal of time while making the movie trying to work out who was the stingier of the two (both showed a remarkable reluctance to pick up the bill after a meal together).

But it has to be said that Hope had other things on his mind at the time – actually two things. One was called Ursula Halloran, who was employed officially as Bob's press agent, but, with a body like hers, had other duties. The other was called Moscow. Bob Hope may have taken a tilt at the Iron Curtain in his movie with Katharine Hepburn, but now he was about to penetrate it. He was going to produce his TV show in Russia. 🅑

BOB HOPE

Chapter Ten - THE ROAD TO MOSCOW

It took a lot to get Bob Hope to Moscow, a great deal of influence, a huge amount of talking and a lot of sweet smiles to the Russian officials, the ones he asked for sixteen visas. In the end, he had to settle for six.

The Russians were more in tune with the wicked capitalist West than might have been thought. They knew all about the troop entertaining he had done and came up with the brilliant idea that he might care to tell jokes to the Soviet troops in Red Square. Ultimately, they agreed that might present a language problem. So they settled for a show starring Russian artists – not at all the sort of thing that NBC normally coupled with the name Bob Hope – which would have to be filmed in Russia and then processed in the Soviet Union, too. They were not taking any chances when it came to propaganda. If Hope tried to implant any anti-Soviet language, they wanted to know about it before the damage was done. The show included excerpts from *Swan Lake* and featured the violinist David Oystrakh.

But the real fun came when Bob entertained the staffs of the American and British embassies. He told the jokes he knew they wanted to hear. Like 'I nearly got arrested when I walked into the Kremlin. I saw a star and thought it was my dressing room.' Or 'They've got a lottery here in Russia – they call it living.' That one was cut from the televised programme that resulted from the show he gave at the embassies. One that remained concerned a subject close to their hearts: their stomachs. 'I know I'm in Russia. This morning my stomach got up two hours before I did and had a bowl of borscht.'

He might not have won any Oscars yet for his movies, but he deserved the Medal of Freedom for tearing down a tiny section of that Iron Curtain. Later, he would be the first American entertainer to be invited to play in Communist China.

Bob Hope – the man now accepted as king of the Republicans in Hollywood, which is not the contradiction in terms it may seem – did more in that TV show to create a kind of normality between East and West than the entire US delegation to the UN had ever achieved. Oh yes, the TV industry liked it, too, and presented him with their Peabody award.

There were so many awards now, it was almost indecent. Queen Elizabeth II noted his contribution to humanity (to say nothing of his British ancestry) and made him an honorary Companion of the Order of the British Empire (CBE).

When the Queen visited America, Bob was there entertaining her. He said that what with the old London Bridge and the *Queen Mary* liner finding new homes in America, it was 'not like you've lost a colony, you've found an attic'.

No one was going to do it better. Where there were troops, Bob and his girls (Ann Sidney, top, and Jill St John, front) would follow. The Far East, 1964.

His next film, *Alias Jesse James* was better than some, but still wasn't Oscar material. It was, though, typical Hope stuff. Who could imagine anyone but Bob playing an insurance salesman who has the lucky break of selling a policy to Jesse James? It wasn't difficult to be convincing as a man with more interest in keeping the outlaw alive than was even James himself.

The Facts of Life was less of a typecasting exercise. In fact, there are a lot of critics who think that in this movie, vaguely based on *Brief Encounter*, he was better than ever before. And once more it was his acting that told. He and Lucille Ball seemed to enjoy every minute of their abortive affair and plainly so did the audience. He told Melville Shavelson that the picture achieved the virtual impossible – it convinced him that 'adultery is very difficult, unless you happen to be British'.

Maybe that was why he always succeeded so well. It was all a matter of his British genes. They didn't, however, do him a lot of good when the seventh and last of the *Road* films was made in Britain. *The Road to Hong Kong* in 1961 was the first indication that Westerners had no future in the colony. Seeing what Bob and Bing made of this trip, any self-respecting Chinese would have wanted to get the island back quick – to prevent anything like it happening again.

Which was plainly the thought of the producers. After *Hong Kong*, the first non-Paramount *Road* venture (it was made by United Artists), there couldn't be another picture to the old formula. Not only were Hope and Crosby not the fellers who had gone to Morocco or Zanzibar, but the things they got up to weren't likely to make the swinging sixties audiences want to laugh. Or even swing.

It was originally going to be called *Road to the Moon*. But the idea of the team cashing in on the current craze for space fiction would only have served to make it out of date from almost the moment it opened in the cinemas. It was still going round the circuits when Yuri Gagarin was going round the earth.

Poor Dorothy Lamour was in orbit much of the time, too – her part disappeared as quickly as a meteor. It is easy to see why she was sidelined to make way for a new female partner, Joan Collins. But she couldn't understand why it was all right for Hope and Crosby to show their years and ostensibly still do what they always did (on screen and off) while she was just there as an attempt to keep the old ship afloat. In fact, it sank – dismally.

I remember interviewing Bob Hope on the *Hong Kong* set at London's Shepperton studios. 'Oh the public will love this,' he told me. 'They'll never grow tired of the *Road* formula.'

He proved himself wrong. In fact, the only thing that really tickled the audience's fancy were the cameo appearances by Frank Sinatra and Dean Martin.

There was another film made in Britain, this time at Pinewood. *Call Me Bwana* had Hope as an explorer who gets drawn into a search for a missing space capsule – he couldn't get away from what was the main preoccupation of the early 1960s.

However, it wasn't *his* main preoccupation. Ask him what was his most enjoyable experience in London at this time and, in a frank mood, he would have admitted it was being a judge at the Miss World contest.

In 1961 an English girl called Rosemary Frankland won the crown – and won Bob, too. He gave her a small part in his films *A Global Affair* and *I'll Take Sweden*. He took her for as long as she was interested and then moved to other pastures.

Ursula Halloran was still on the scene, but, when she took to drink, Bob sacked her both from her job as press agent and as number-one mistress. The drink became an even greater problem for her and before long she was complicating it with drugs. Soon, she was dead from an overdose. Bob flew to her funeral. It was an unhappy experience for him. Ursula's sister, a nun, saw him in the congregation and started verbally abusing him in the chapel. He flew back from Pittsburgh, more shaken by this than by anything else that had ever happened to him.

But there was always something to put him back on course. The television shows were bigger than ever. So was the amount of national adulation. Bob was having serious eye trouble now, constantly in hospital or receiving treatment, but it seemed to clear up and he wasn't going to let it affect the number of times he was presented with awards. There were hundreds of them now. The trophy room at the Toluca Lake house was expanding into a veritable museum. Nobody who was invited to the house failed to stray into the room with its collection of medals, awards, certificates and city freedoms.

'I don't take those seriously,' he said. 'I was rung up once by a man in Atlanta who said he was going to proclaim June 6 as Bob Hope Day and would I come for the ceremony. I said, "Wait a minute, let's look at my diary. No June 6. I'm abroad." There was silence for the minute and then the mayor said, "Do you have Red Skelton's number?"'

That, he thought, put the award business in perspective – although Jan King was quoted by Arthur Marx as saying that she was at one time told to solicit more and more of those awards.

She didn't have anything to do with the one that President Kennedy presented him in 1962. Bob at last did get the Medal of Freedom at a White House ceremony. Kennedy told him that he was America's Prized Ambassador of Goodwill. 'It's been one of the rarest honours given to Americans and it's a great pleasure for me on behalf of the Congress to present this to you – it's got a lovely picture of you – on behalf of the people of the United States.' To which Bob replied, 'Thank you Mr President. I suggested to Senator Symington that I ought to have had a nose job. but he said then it would have been less gold. Actually ... I feel very humble – although I think I have the strength of character to fight it.'

Dolores was with him at the ceremony, laughing and enjoying seeing her husband being fêted again by an American President. At home, she worried more and more about the rivals for her bed. She wasn't the only one who worried. Now

BOB HOPE

John F. Kennedy presented Bob with a medal. He wondered if he ought to have had a nose job.

her mother, Theresa, was recruited to the cause. She had friends spy on her son-in-law and on one celebrated occasion listened in on a telephone conversation between Bob and a woman. 'She was so engrossed,' Jan King told me, 'that she fell back down the stairs and broke her hip.' His younger daughter Nora was another one of the spies. King told me, 'When she got her driving licence she said, "Now I can follow Daddy at night" – and Bob said, "She's my little FBI".'

Nora might have been worried about the return of Marilyn Maxwell into her father's life, although there is no reason to believe that, when she featured in his movie *Critics' Choice* in 1963, her role was any more than just professional. The real co-star was Lucille Ball again and there had never been any bedtime romance with her. There certainly was little romance about the film. You only have to imagine the idea of Bob Hope playing a theatre critic – one forced by his sense of integrity to give his wife's play a bad review – to wonder about the wisdom of the casting. The critic Judith Crist seemed to sum up the reaction of most people who saw it. She called it 'instant stultification'.

So had he lost his movie touch? The truth now was that Hope was so keen on making enough dollars to maintain his ever-growing reputation as the richest man in Hollywood that he was only interested in the figures on a studio contract . *I'll Take Sweden* just wasn't worth it mainly because Hope took control of the intelligent script and insisted on inserting a scene that had nothing to do with the plot at all – which goes to show just how powerful he still was.

Arthur Marx refused to agree to the scene being added. The film was completed – with the extra scene, which at least Hope thought useful and funny.

As for *A Global Affair*, again it was a movie whose title was more appropriate to him than the plot. This time he was a UN official who had to look after an abandoned baby. Arthur Marx would have benefited by having another star playing the part. In fact, Bob himself would have benefited even before now by quitting his film career while he was still ahead. Or was he still ahead? He went on making the pictures that benefited only his bank account.

Surprisingly, *Boy, Did I Get A Wrong Number* did *not* refer to the call he made to his agent when he agreed to make this 1965 movie about a real-estate man who gets involved with a runaway actress. He would have been better advised to have put the phone down. The one redeeming feature was the presence in the movie of Phyllis Diller, who told me she thought she had begun to take the place of Bing Crosby in Bob's life. Except, she said, 'I am no golfer. So I became a caddie and dressed up funny because he loved laughs. I learned almost everything I know about comedy from him.' She was constantly on the TV shows, and cooked for him at her own parties, when they would just sit and laugh at each other.

The zany comedienne, who looked not just as though she had been dragged through a bush backwards but as though she *was* the bush, told me about working with Hope. 'He used to say that my bra size was a thirty-four long.'

Janis Paige relived her Korea experiences by appearing regularly on Bob's TV show. She had been doing it ever since they made Hope's first ever colour broadcast from New York to the West Coast – an experiment Bob himself didn't like very much. He was one of the last stars to agree to their black-and-white shows being transmitted in colour, which he thought put too much of a strain on performers. New kinds of make-up, lighting and sets took it to a stage where it was virtually a new medium altogether – and, really, there had been too many of those already.

Of course, when he succumbed, he wanted every new development that was available. In 1969, he thought it was a good time to revive one of the great experiences in his life – doing a TV version of *Roberta* with Janis . They filmed it at Southern Memphis University in Dallas and it was a huge success – so successful that it was repeated: the two did another version ten years later.

But when the first *Roberta* was televised he also had other things on his mind. America was ever more deeply involved in the Vietnam war. To Bob Hope that was the bugle call. He got up, dusted himself down and got the gang together. 🔵

Chapter Eleven – CANCEL MY RESERVATION

Vietnam was the Great American Tragedy. In a way, it would prove to be Bob Hope's tragedy, too. But it also showed a Hope more giving, more brave, and in some ways more funny than he had ever been before. 'What a welcome I got at the airport – they thought I was a replacement. I understand that the enemy is very close – well, with my act, they always are. I asked Secretary McNamara if I could be of any help. He said, "Why not? We've tried everything else".'

And he admitted it was terrible country for a coward. 'Can you imagine my not knowing which way to run!' But he said he'd keep running – to the next base – until the war was over and still he said he was scared all the way down his ski-slope nose. 'You heard of the NBC peacock? This is a Far-Eastern chicken.'

He barnstormed his way from one end of the country to the other, making friends of generals, but living always with the enlisted men – and warning the enemy: 'If there are any Viet Cong in the audience, I've already got my shots.'

Mel Shavelson recalled his fellow writer Mort Lachman trying to persuade Bob at one show to move to one side. Hope was mystified. Afterwards, Lachman explained. 'The jokes weren't playing.' It was actually the Viet Cong – who were not just playing, either. Lachman spotted a group of North Vietnamese pointing towards the stage. Janis Paige remembers the incident well. 'There was a mortar aimed at us.' Perhaps they were impressed with the jokes – they didn't actually get as far as shooting.

At first, America was with him, just as, it has to be admitted, a swathe of America was behind the war. But then – and very quickly – things began to change. There was a massacre at My-Lai and young men started burning their draft cards. Bob carried on as though he had a self-appointed mission to proclaim the patriotism of the nation.

A lot had to do with the fact that he still believed that his President was always right. Crowds might be shouting outside the White House, 'Hey, hey, LBJ – how many boys did you kill today?' He may have been a dedicated Republican, honorary patron of all the Palm Springs Republicans who joined him at the Rancho Mirage country club to proclaim the justice of big business, but he thought the Democrat Lyndon Baines Johnson had the right to expect real Americans to rally to the colours, even if those colours were now drab, dirty and bloodstained.

When he appeared before the men, he gave them his message: 'I've been reading about the My-Lai massacre. That's all you read in the headlines, not about

With Gerry Ford. He always loved being with the President. Any President – especially if he played golf.

the good things you guys have been doing. You know, the sacrifice. They say they're all so anti-war and think that the reason I come over here is because I'm pro-war. Let me tell you something: this is the thirtieth year I've been doing this and there's nobody more anti-war than I am and nobody more anti-war than you.' He was cheered and whistled at.

Of course, for a long time, the Americans weren't actually fighting in Vietnam. They were there as 'advisers'. So he'd begin his shows by saying, 'Good evening, advisers!' It was one of the few jokes he made about that undeclared war – which he said in *Don't shoot* was a real war with real, undeclared bullets.

He was taken into the military's confidence. A general showed him the battle plan. There were going to be attacks on this sector and more on that place and there were plans to fly over the area to the north. 'In that case,' said Bob, 'I'll stay for lunch.'

Later, he told Bob Thomas, a Hollywood biographer and Associated Press writer, 'This is important to the world. Listen – if the Commies ever thought we weren't going to protect the Vietnamese, there would be Vietnams everywhere. That would be a lot worse than what we're facing now. Like it or not, we're the Big Daddy of the Free World.'

And he was not just the Big Daddy of the entertainment world, but cock o' the walk of every nest of hawks you could find. *Variety* reported his saying that he expected 'something big to happen soon. Maybe not THE BOMB, but crippling air strikes in hot pursuit of the enemy into bordering neutral countries.'

He was even quoted by a *Life* magazine reporter as telling a meeting at Flint, Michigan, that he thought the war was 'a beautiful thing – we paid in a lot of gorgeous American lives, but we're not sorry for it.' He later denied the quote. It was the first indication that perhaps he ought to have second thoughts about the *kind* of sentiment he had been expressing.

But, when things were going wrong, he could still joke about it. 'And I love this place. Great golfing country. Even the runway has eighteen holes.' Not only that, they gave him a twenty-one-gun salute. 'Three of them were ours.'

Melville Shavelson was back with his NAFTs, providing a whole clutch of stories made to measure for the situation.

There were those who wondered how any human being could be funny in the face of so much misery. He saw the napalm bombings and survived shells that burst in the middle of shows. No one could doubt that his bravery was outstanding. If it was suggested that he go up in one of the gunships that were strafing nearly all the Vietcong-occupied territory and put on a show for the crew between blasts of their machine guns, he'd have done it. And, unlike almost everything else he did, he would have done so for free, even without a TV camera to film the event. (Although as Les Brown said, 'The ratings were so immense with the Christmas show we did from there that Bob said, "Let's do it again next year".')

The Department of Defence supplied the planes that took Hope and his party from one base to the next. Janis Paige, who was in the party on a number of the Vietnam trips – and there would be nine of them – told me about the escort the military provided for them. 'We'd look out the window and there were fighter planes alongside our planes. I got a little bit nervous and they peeled off. They were so close, you could look out the window and you could see their faces and wave to them.'

He tended to behave himself with the women from this group, Jan King was quoted as telling *The Globe* for their 1991 article. He preferred 'exotic local ladies' like the woman, 'seductively' dressed in a skin-tight miniskirt and a low-cut blouse that revealed most of her bosom. Although she later denied it, Jan was reported to have said that his particular exotic lady led Hope up to her room, after meeting him at the bar.

There's no doubt that he went to Vietnam because he knew he was doing good for the men. That has to be said over and over again. 'I do think he had a dual reason for doing it,' said Les Brown. 'He was actually the entertainer who wanted to take care of more GIs than any other entertainers in the business. He loved working with GIs. He loved the GI audience.' And that went for his co-stars. When Jerry Colonna had a stroke, Phyllis Diller replaced him. She told me: 'Bob taught me how to manage those hospital visits. The first one [we went to] I dissolved in tears and actually was no good at all. It was very dangerous, but I don't think he was a man who worried about death.'

If he had worried about them, he wouldn't still be able to make jokes about the position they were all in. He didn't excuse the food they were eating from his strictures. As he said once: 'We threw the box lunches overboard and watched the sharks get sick.'

He invited along to his shows celebrities to whom he thought this all-important audience could relate. Once astronaut Neil Armstrong shared the stage with him.

Frances Langford put it like this: 'I think he found out that this was so much of what he really wanted to do for his country – and I think we all felt this way.'

The most dangerous situation of all was averted mainly because of Bob's dependence on his idiot cards. As always, Barney McNully was on hand on this trip, listening to the writers, talking over the planned script with Hope and then rushing to the boards with his black marker pen. When Bob came on stage, Barney was there at the prearranged position – to follow his master's eye, dashing from one end of the auditorium to the other, always remembering to stay out of camera range. (Yes, he was going to make money and get exposure from the trip, but there *were* easier ways of making that money and getting that exposure.)

There were three things about Barney's reputation that were well known to the members of the entourage: his devotion to Bob, their mutual affection and the fact that Barney was always late. It normally didn't matter, but on this occasion, the team were tired and wanted to get back to Saigon, where they were due to stay at the Caravelle Hotel. They also had to wend their way through a hail of sniper fire – and Barney *was* late. They didn't like him at all at that moment. Eventually they got to a shattered Caravelle to find that the hotel opposite the Brinks had been totally wrecked, two soldiers were killed and dozens injured.

'Bob always said that after that I could do no wrong,' said Barney. 'If we weren't late, we could all have been killed.' Janis Paige told me, 'We saw the smoke curling up from the airport. When we got there, there was smashed glass and devastation all over. I remember being shoved through the door of the hotel where we were staying and taken up to my room and told to stay there. We were bomb-checked twice a day. A bomb squad would come and check the toilets. It was extremely dangerous. But we weren't aware of it. We were too busy. We worked and worked and worked. You did not stop.'

Bob always claimed that the Vietcong were actually trying to get at him – and for once was not joking. The heat was terrible. Bob had some serious eye trouble again. (Doctors knew that it had been caused by a cerebral haemorrhage that resulted from a fall while entertaining more troops in Iceland – a strong woman had dropped him on his head.) 'I saw him irritable,' said Janis Paige. 'But I realize, looking back, that he wasn't feeling well.' Like others, she saw him tour the hospitals. Once, he left a soldier's bedside with blood over his suit. He got that close.

Hope came home from that trip and went back to make more TV shows and appear as a cameo in a movie cruelly called *The Oscar*. There was no chance of his getting the coveted award himself now – at least, not for a movie of his own, but in 1965, the Academy did present him with a medal. There had now been five honorary academic prizes, including two Oscars and the Jean Hersholt humanitarian award.

And there was the continual run of beauty competitions. In 1968, he was a judge at that year's Miss World USA contest – won by Johnine Avery, with whom he subsequently became friendly. The United Press International report of the contest noted that Jade Hagen, of Kansas, claimed that the win was a fraud and that she was seeing a lawyer.

Arthur Marx told me that there was one other cloud on the Avery–Hope horizon. Johnine, who had been on a number of Hope TV shows, went on Bing Crosby's programme when Bob was abroad. That was disloyalty of the highest order, especially at a time when Hope was constantly nursing the sores that arose from less than enthusiastic reviews of his movies.

Eight On The Lam, the story of a bank clerk charged with embezzlement, was terrible. The relationship with Johnine ended soon after that. So, too, it seemed, did Bob Hope's career as everyone's favourite comedian. 'The star [has] lost his comic character,' said Leslie Halliwell, author of the famous Film Guides. He

Sammy Davies Jnr, Richard Nixon, Les Brown and Bob. There had never been a 'ticket' like that before. 1973.

certainly didn't find it with *The Private Navy of Sgt. O'Farrell* in 1968, although Phyllis Diller tried to help him back to his old form.

Both Diller and Bob thought they were on safer ground when they were ready to go back to Vietnam. The shows followed the same style as ever, although the jokes were new. Sometimes newer than anyone would imagine. 'I hear you fellows are interested in gardening,' said Bob at one performance. 'Our CO tells us you grow a lot of grass.'

He was convinced the troops liked him – no, he felt they *loved* him – as much as ever before. But there were people who were not so enthusiastic. Sometimes, the reception was as great as it had ever been. At others, the men looked tired, sick and in no more mood to laugh than they were to unload more napalm.

It was a situation that had radiated from the firing line back to the United States. The people who loved him at the beginning of the decade now grouped him together with Johnson and Nixon. There were those who were even calling the conflict 'Hope's War'.

He was unrepentant. 'I have got news for you,' he told one audience,'the country is behind you – 50 per cent.' There was bitterness inside him now. But that wasn't the hardest problem with the way he was working. Mel Shavelson told me that it was meeting a group of American youngsters that brought about the big change. 'He became something of a joke. I said to him, "This is not a joke. This is not something that the public would want to see you do".'

Bob surprised him with his response: 'I was in Washington last week,' he told Shavelson, 'and I was outside the hotel putting my golf clubs in my car when a convertible with a lot of fellows in it drove by and one of them said to met "Hey Bob, we're gonna bring them home to *you* this Christmas".'

That was the end of the Vietnam shows. 'And it was Bob's realization that most of them were laughing in a situation in which they knew they might not survive,' Shavelson continued. 'While, certainly, he was cheering them up, he was taking advantage of the situation. Now he didn't want to be accused of promoting something terrible which he would be accused of continuing.'

When he spoke to the students at the Catholic Notre Dame University, he was booed. So different from another occasion at the college. Then, they cheered as he told them he was so glad to be back at the college founded by Pat O'Brien (the actor who had played so many priests in those early Warner Brothers movies and had starred in the title role of *Knute Rockne*, the legendary Notre Dame football coach). He had been in very good form that night. The jokes rattled out like all the prizes he was getting. Notre Dame presented him with their Patriotism Award. He told them:'Before I say another word, I have a confession – and this is a pretty good place to have one, isn't it?' He said he hadn't felt so good since the government had let him declare Bing Crosby as a dependant. He wondered if he had got their award for paying his taxes – or for leaving the country so often.

As ever, it was the opinion of his President that counted above all others. When Richard Nixon finally brought the troops out of Vietnam, he said he was glad. He himself had wanted to get out, he protested. 'I was a hawk in Vietnam for as long as there was a chance to win that war. I wanted to win – just like every kid I entertained out there. They wanted to win and to get home. When it got to the point that they weren't going to win, I wanted to see those kids get back. It was a tough deal.'

Whether Vietnam was responsible we can't really be sure, but the unstoppable popularity of Bob Hope was now ebbing. New, grittier comedians had come on the scene. Woody Allen had abandoned his hilarious night club act to make his first movies and Mel Brooks had discovered a gold mine in a totally new concept involving a 2,000-year-old man, and after *The Producers*, which introduced a new kind of film comedy altogether, went on to prove his original mastery in a whole succession of movies. Lenny Bruce and Mort Sahl were telling a different kind of joke that people like Hope never found funny – American youngsters were saying out loud that they preferred their sort of humour. They also preferred their politics, which were right at the other extreme from the stance Hope took.

Nevertheless, his films continued to make money. As ever, their titles were strangely pertinent to Hope's personal life. *How To Commit Marriage* could have been a lesson in having a wife without complicating your sex activities. It was, however, described as a 'generation-gap comedy'. The gap was more between Hope and his audience, many of whom didn't think it was a comedy at all. But there was always a loyal following.

One of the last public acts of Richard Nixon was to host a banquet at the White House for returning prisoners of war. Bob was guest of honour. The only blight on the occasion was that it came in the midst of the Watergate scandal. Even Hope didn't joke about that – at the time.

Then Gerald Ford took over the presidency.There was no Vietnam to worry about any more – except the continual soul-searching of the American people as they read and saw on their TV screens the horror of the bombings and the deaths of young people who had never wanted to go there in the first place. It was the first war in which no one could adequately justify the part that their country had played. When Americans saw maimed youngsters struggling in wheelchairs or on crutches, the picture became even stronger.

Hope said nothing more about it for years. But he kept up his relationship with his President – whoever he was. He played golf with Gerald Ford, which he enjoyed – because Ford wasn't such a good player and there was always money on the game. 'It's always good to get something back from the government,' he joked.

At about this time, a group of wealthy Republicans lobbied to have Bob himself run for President – ignoring the fact that the American Constitution banned anyone from the top job who had not been born in the United States. In any case, Hope said he wasn't interested. 'The money's not right,' he explained. 'Only two hundred thousand dollars – what would my wife have to spend in the second week?' Then he added, 'Besides, I wouldn't want to move to a smaller house.'

Nevertheless, all things considered, the real problem was that running for election would mean having to be on the campaign trail for six or seven weeks. 'And I'm not used to being home for so long.'

What was more, there was something distinctly unsavoury about the electoral process. As he joked, 'People are out in their gardens, spreading the same stuff as the political candidates.' But, he said, he knew he would have fun addressing the nation. He would introduce himself in the old presidential style: 'Good evening, ladies and gentlemen. This is Bob "Chief Executive" Hope.'

It seemed as if the Presidents were the only really loyal audience he still had. The moviegoers were staying away in their hundreds of thousands now. *Cancel My Reservation* – which in a way, seemed an appropriate title for a man who was no longer sure he still was on the Road To Never-Ending Success – was even worse than the other movies he had been making recently. The film was a sorry result of too many cooks involving themselves in writer Arthur Marx's broth. It might have been a good story – about a talk-show host who gets involved in a murder – but so many people wanted a slice of the action, including Hope and a clutch of writers he brought in to add and subtract from the original screenplay, it was terrible.

Apart from a cameo performance in a Muppet film and a film made specially for television, it was to be Hope's last movie. It's one of the saddest features of the Bob Hope story – that the supreme master of timing hadn't realized years before that the time had come to go out on a high note.

Maybe he hadn't discovered that there was a difference between the audiences who saw him in the comfort of their homes and those who paid for their movie tickets. He plainly made television his priority and after all, he had been on the small screen for a long time. As he remarked, 'When I began, *TV Guide* had one page.'

His stance over Vietnam had done a lot of harm to his reputation. But then something strange happened – strange to him and to a lot of the observers of the entertainment scene. *Teenage* magazine voted him 'The Most Popular Man In America'. Second was John Travolta. 'I think those kids must have been on something,' he joked. Certainly, not everyone joined in those tributes. In 1975, the fight was still simmering. Hope got himself involved in the nastiest ever Oscar ceremony, and stepped right into the middle of a historic row.

The award for the best documentary went that year to Peter Davis, one of the two producers of *Hearts and Minds*, which was about the Vietnam war. Davis made a speech condemning the war. Then the other producer, Bert Schneider, spoke about his joy at Vietnam being 'liberated'. There were buzzes in the audience. John Wayne cried 'Shame'. Bob demanded – loudly – that the president of the Academy, Howard W. Koch, make a speech dissociating the Academy from the speeches. Then he persuaded Frank Sinatra to make the speech – which became a row in itself because Sinatra, unlike Hope, had at one time had a reputation for being the great Hollywood liberal. Sinatra did make the speech, reading an apology that had been crafted by Bob – and not one of his writers – and Hope became his newest and most devoted fan.

The 1978 Miss World show in London, at which he was the star turn, was even worse. It was a combination of antipathy to his Vietnam stand and – in this case, much more seriously – his backing for something deemed so politically incorrect as a beauty contest. The whole affair turned into a disaster.

A group of feminist demonstrators interrupted the TV showing of the event, throwing flour and smoke bombs everywhere – and, even worse, knocking down Bob's idiot cards. He tried to joke it off, but he had never looked so flustered.

The audiences to his TV specials – and because there were fewer of them, just four a year, every one became a special – got smaller and his sponsors changed from time to time. But there was still a respectable enough crowd out there wanting to see Hope to make it worth NBC's while to continue airing the shows – and for the big stars to still want to appear.

They were glossier than ever, but the content wasn't always that way. He and John Wayne got together on one show – and used precisely the same script that they had worked from in the old black-and–white days, twenty-odd years before.

TV and golf were now taking up nearly all of his time, although there would always be the Christmas shows to troops stationed in uncontroversial places like Greenland or Australia.

Bob occupied himself with more and more golf and more and more land deals. And with always being the most popular guest on talk shows when he wasn't planning one of his own. When he appeared on the Michael Parkinson show on BBC television in 1980, he was seventy-seven years of age. He looked at least ten

The family man. With Dolores (left) celebrating 25 years of marriage and daughter Linda (right).

years younger. By then, he had been told that his ocular problems were getting much worse and before long he would lose the sight of that damaged eye, but you'd never have noticed it as he talked golf and discussed the situation in his own profession.

It was the time Hollywood's top actors had been joining picket lines in solidarity with less successful actors who were demanding residual payments for television reruns of their movies and TV shows. Hope the arch-conservative was in his element. 'It's a funny kind of strike when people can go straight from a picket line, get into their Rolls-Royces and then drive to their big homes with the swimming pools – and say they're not going back to work until they have improved working conditions.' As he said, 'Everyone was picketing from their good side. It was the first time I ever saw a picket line with a maître d.'

It was all a matter of politics, although sometimes Bob thought his political influence was stronger than it was. When, in 1980, Jimmy Carter failed to get the American hostages held in the Tehran embassy released by revolutionaries in Iran, he offered to go over to the country and entertain there while a deal was arranged. The idea of the ayotollahs being moved by Bob Hope may sound ridiculous, but serious talks did take place with Hope speaking directly to the Iranians on the one hand and to the White House on the other.

Carter thought that, since everything else had been tried, it was worth making the effort. After all, he trusted Bob. A few years earlier on Bob's seventy-fifth birthday he had led the tributes to his favourite comedian. Carter had been in office for 489 days, he said: 'Three weeks more and I'll have stayed in the White

BOB HOPE

The Presidents' man – again. L-R: Dwight Eisenhower, Bob, Ronald Reagan and Arnold Palmer.

House as many times as Bob Hope.' To which Bob returned his thanks for the hospitality of the presidential mansion. 'God knows, we've paid for it.'

He liked Carter, but when Ronald Reagan entered the fray for the presidency, there was no contest as to whom he was going to support. Or joke about. If only his old pal had been listening. He said people had been telling Reagan to get a hearing aid for a long time, but he couldn't hear what they were saying. Reagan joked that he and Hope once shared a box at a theatre with two seats in it. One seat was marked 'Out-of-work movie actor', the other, 'America's Best-loved Citizen'. They fought for the seat they thought more flattering.

Bob and Reagan played golf and even did a double act together. 'I want to tell you, Mr President,' said Hope, 'that with all the work and the travelling you do, you look just great.'

'You look great,too,' said Reagan. At which point they said in unison, 'I hope I look as good as you when I'm your age.' There are not many countries where you can joke like that with the President, which may be one of the reasons Bob Hope stayed an American and didn't take that job emceeing at a salt mine. That and the golf. And the money.

When George Bush was about to take the oath for the presidency, Hope gagged that everyone was wondering whether he would pronounce the sacred words or merely ask the American people to 'Read my lips'. Bush had reason to be grateful for Bob. When the Gulf War broke out in 1991, Hope went back to his favourite audience. Dressed in camouflage fatigues, the man who was close to being a nonagenarian still managed to sing a couple of choruses of 'Thanks For The Memory' and joke, 'What the Israelis did in six days, you guys can do in three.'

That was fighting talk, but that was what those guys expected. It was good for his TV career. NBC broadcast extracts from the concert and called it *Bob Hope's Christmas Cheer In Saudi Arabia*.

The astonishing thing was that he was still working at all and still able to read those idiot cards, although the letters now had to be a foot high and be held by Barney McNulty at precisely the right height and distance.

Barney was still an essential fixture in Bob's life. The TV host Steve Allen told me about one particular showbiz party he had attended. He said everything came to a halt when Bob walked in. He was mobbed – and then he made a speech. 'He was very, very funny and witty,' said Allen. 'The party was in the open air and I found myself following his eyeline. I saw that he was looking into a far corner. And there, hiding in the bushes, was Barney – with his cue cards.'

Hope was still very much a business man. His daughter Linda was deputed to run his showbusiness interests as head of his corporation. But he knew what was going on – particularly with his property deals. There could be nothing old hat about either buying or selling land. An arrangement had to be as up to date as one of his jokes – the current market value. In 1985, the National Park Service wanted to take over his Jordan Ranch in the Santa Monica mountains. Bob knew how much the service wanted it. He haggled with them for months – suggesting at one time that they trade a piece of land. The only problem was that his plot was not only inaccessible – it was wanted precisely because it would be used for a road – it was also barren.

After months and months of arguments – and a great deal of criticism in the media – he agreed to sell, not exchange. His price, $16.7 million, was much more than he would have got on the open market.

It's a story that he would have loved to have talked over with Bing, but Crosby had died on a golf course in Spain seven years before. With him died Hope's last big ambition – to make yet another *Road* film. Mel Shavelson had presented them with a script that they had both liked, called *The Road To The Fountain of Youth*. (They had previously planned a *Road to Moscow* but the studio were not keen on any attempt to breach the Iron Curtain at the time.)

The death of Crosby made Bob want to be even more busy, although not totally successfully. He looked for new opportunities – even to make *The Road To The Fountain of Youth*, this time with George Burns. But Lew Grade, who wanted to produce it, demanded a five-year deal to pay the money Burns demanded. George, then eighty-five, didn't feel like waiting.

Chapter Twelve - NOTHIN' BUT THE TRUTH

So what made Bob Hope, a man with so many human frailties, so loved? The answer has a lot to do with those very frailties. Audiences saw in him a man who for most of his life not only joked about what was going on in their world, but one who had so obviously lived in that world, too.

The Vietnam war took a long time to live down and, in many people's minds, Bob's stance on the conflict made it just as long before he could become acceptable again. In the end, war fever cooled and they forgave him for it. Just as they forgave what he was serving them on TV. The memories were still things for which they wanted to give thanks and became even more important as his physical appearance increasingly betrayed the years.

In his eighties, he made television programmes that seemed highly inappropriate – like singing love songs to the almost juvenile Brooke Shields, as he did in his eightieth-birthday programme in 1984. Much more right for him was the duet he did at the age of ninety with Angela Lansbury, dancing quite well to a specially written version of Cole Porter's 'Well Did You Evah'. It was the first time they had even met, but they hammed it up like the troupers they both were, as though they had been doing it all their lives. It was what people wanted to see, Hope not so much acting his age, but showing that he was still a star. So many of his specials had not just been very poor but had been no credit to him at all. In the Brooke Shields programme, Bob, his hair dyed and wearing a false moustache, did a duet with Placido Domingo, both playing Mississippi riverboat men, which neither of them did well.

One of the most embarrassing Hope performances came for British television in 1994 – when the D-Day landings of fifty years earlier were commemorated. Bob was heading an all-star cast from the *Queen Elizabeth II*, moored off Southampton. He couldn't remember his lines or read the cue cards. The programme was interrupted 'due to a breakdown in the link'.

And yet the overpowering fact was that he actually didn't *have* to be very good any more. It just didn't matter. The realization that it was still Bob Hope there on the screen and that Bob Hope was still alive somehow was enough. When he went on those shows, it was plain that he was still not just liked but loved by the people who saw them. And, while they were nothing like the audiences he had once commanded, there was still a very respectable loyal public who really loved him.

Back in England with the owners of the house in which Bob was born. 1980.

BOB HOPE

Still the girls' favourite. Lucille Ball and Brooke Shields join in the kissing game. 1986.

Extreme old age had suddenly descended and with a vengeance. The man who never looked his years now looked all of them. He pretended that he was still in command of his faculties, but his blind eye made him look worse than he might otherwise have seemed.

His producer, Elliot Kozak, had never known whether he was working with Bob from one season to another. After nearly twenty years, Bob told him that he was making changes. He was going to ask Mel Shavelson to produce a show for him.

Kozak liked Bob and does so to this day. His failure to tell him till the last minute that he was out of work – 'and I had made a lot of money from him' – was due to one indisputable fact, he said: Hope was a coward. 'He has many friends and wouldn't do anything to harm them. But he cannot bear illness. His agent Jimmy Shurr was dying of cancer, brain cancer, and he never went to see him in hospital. He doesn't want to be near anything like that. Possibly, he was just frightened of what lay ahead.'

Bob Hope continued to make those TV specials until NBC, not Bob himself, decided in 1996 not to renew his contract. For the first time since the 1930s he had neither a radio nor a television agreement guaranteeing him new opportunities to make a fortune.

He was suffering from that great curse of super old age – he had outlived almost everyone he had known during his glory years. Dolores was still vibrantly active. In 1997 she brought out her own CD, singing her favourite songs. But she and the children were the only ones close to him now. His brothers had died – along with Bing, Dorothy Lamour and Jerry Colonna.

But nobody could doubt that he himself would always be remembered. The earlier films, the records of his best radio programmes and his lyrical voice singing those hits of the 1940s, and the earlier TV shows were all proofs for posterity of how important and talented he had been. And there were other memorials of his importance around, too. Palm Springs, although he had stopped enjoying living there, was a virtual Hope shrine. One of its main arteries was called Bob Hope Drive – hence all the big signs on roads in the Rancho Mirage area that just proclaimed in big green letters the words 'Bob Hope'. The Eisenhower Medical Center had wings named after him and Dolores. You couldn't live in that part of the world and pretend you had never heard the name Bob Hope.

He had done so much. He was the man who said on his 90th birthday: 'If I had my life to live over again, I wouldn't have the time.' But words on plaques and street signs couldn't be enough. Golf and the TV commercial for K-Mart were really all that was left for him. The days when he could say, 'The best year of my life is next year,' were now over. More likely was the other quote attributed to him,' I guess God had something in mind for us because we're still hanging around.'

The man who once boasted a handicap of four could still say that golf was the one real passion in his life. In December 1997, a magazine picture appeared of a dapper-looking Bob Hope (he hadn't looked like that for at least thirty years) advertising the 'Special Edition Bob Hope putter' with both his signature and his ski-slope nose at the dangerous end. 'Golf is my real profession,' he was quoted as saying. 'Entertainment is just a sideline. I tell jokes to pay my greens fees.'

The real joke was that he would have carried on until he literally dropped. Even Bill Clinton came to pay Bob tribute when NBC aired Hope's last TV show in 1996 – when Bob said that at last he was 'a free agent'. He could take up other people's offers now. That was when he revealed that the one big perk of his job was playing golf with Bob. The programme segment was called 'Laughing With The Presidents' – and showed clips of Bob entertaining eleven of them.

Looking at just how old Hope was, you might be tempted to think that the list of presidents began with Abraham Lincoln. But these days, Franklin Roosevelt is going back far enough. 'I know the Presidents liked my jokes,' he once said. 'The taxman told me when he came to take away my garage.' No President would dare do anything of the kind. If he did, the American armed forces would have had something to say about it.

The network had by then thought that the time had come. In that last show, there was an MC taking up much of the time and the Presidents were pretty good co-stars who filled up most of the rest. In the end, Hope had to be helped down the corridor, the setting for the last scene. He walked arm in arm with the MC and you saw them – from the back – disappearing around a corner. The true fans would hope that there was something symbolic in that – maybe there *was* something

Bob as he would like to be remembered. Still smiling.

exciting round the corner. It could only have been wishful thinking. The nonagenarian Hope was honoured by the men in uniform for whom he had done so much. The Navy named a ship, the second largest in the fleet, the 'USNS Bob Hope'. At almost the same time, the Air Force named a plane 'The Spirit of Bob Hope'.

But what of that spirit? Mel Shavelson told me that he met Bob at a Hollywood function and his old boss didn't even know who he was. He had very slight vision and practically no hearing to go along with his lost memory.

His family, now secure in the knowledge that he would be staying home, encouraged Bob to be active. He still took part in the odd TV interview, fed the lines through an ultra-powerful hearing aid. But even that didn't work. On one show, he was supposedly 'interviewing' the former First Lady, Barbara Bush. She had to give him his questions during hurriedly arranged commercial breaks.

Similarly, watching Bob play golf was, according to your viewpoint, either a sorry sight or a wonderful tribute to his continuing endurance. He would no longer make jokes to people he played with – like the man who asked him what the stakes would be. 'Do you own your own car?' asked Bob. He would sit in the clubroom at the Rancho Mirage waiting for his name to be called. Two big men would then lift him to the first tee and tell him where the ball was. 'But you know,' a friend told me, 'on the course he is suddenly Bob Hope again. It's as though he has been fed a dose of adrenalin.'

He probably still felt that way whenever someone told him there was a camera pointing his way – even if he couldn't see it. As Carrol Baker, the former *Baby Doll* star who went with him to Vietnam, told me, 'His life has been in show business and show business *is* his life.'

But the honours still tumbled in like the daily post. In 1997 President Bill Clinton declared him an 'Honorary Veteran'. Of course he had been a veteran performer for longer than anyone could remember, but this meant that all his years of service to the fighting men of America was finally recognised. It also meant, that should he fall on hard times when he got *really* old, he could claim benefits.

Then, early the next year, Britain honoured its native son again. He became an honorary knight. If he changed his nationality back to the one with which he was born, that would have made him Sir Bob. But it would never happen. He would never forsake America, the country he more than anyone else made smile. As Milton Berle put it: 'I always said that Bob Hope had class – with a capital 'K'.'

Hope himself always said that his maxim was: 'When you hear an audience laugh, it's therapy'. It would be nice to think that there is enough therapy out there for him still to be able to say 'Thanks for the memory'. ⏍

PHOTOGRAPHS